To Walk as HE Walked

T.B. MASTON

D1249925

BROADMAN PRESS
Nashville, Tennessee

© Copyright 1985 • Broadman Press
All rights reserved
4250-24
ISBN: 0-8054-5024-6
Dewey Decimal Classification: 232.954
Subject Heading: JESUS CHRIST—TEACHINGS
Library of Congress Catalog Card Number: 85-17173
Printed in the United States of America

Library of Congress Cataloging-in-Publication Data

Maston, T. B. (Thomas Bufford), 1897-
    To walk as He walked.

    Bibliography: p.
    1. Jesus Christ—Character. 2. Christian ethics—Baptist authors. 3. Christian life—Baptist authors.
I. Title
BT304.M34   1985   232.9′03   85-17173
ISBN 0-8054-5024-6 (pbk.)

To my and Mommie's parents
Samuel H. and Sarah Sellers Maston
and
Thomas C. and Cassandra Stockburger McDonald

Acknowledgments

Several friends contributed in various ways to this book. Among those who checked the prospectus for the book, including possible chapter titles, outlines, and the like, were Derrell Watkins and Elmer West. James Dunn, J. W. MacGorman, and Leon Marsh read and critically evaluated the final typescript. Leon Marsh had also checked the original prospectus. All of these men took time from busy schedules to read and evaluate the manuscript. They caught a number of errors and also made several suggestions that have contributed to a more readable and accurate volume. It should be understood, of course, that I alone am responsible for the final form of the book, including any errors and mistakes in interpretation.

A special word of appreciation should be expressed to Dora Etta Bridgford who not only made the final typescript but who also, as she has so often done previously, made the original typewritten copy from my poorly handwritten pages.

A special word of appreciation should be expressed to my wife, "Mommie." She and I have walked together for many years. She reveals as much of the spirit of Jesus in relation to people who are hurting and the underprivileged in general as anyone I know.

Preface

Throughout Christian history, believers have tended to neglect either the human nature or the divine nature of Jesus. All of us are grateful that Jesus was and is Christ, the Son of God and our Lord and Savior. "There is salvation in no one else, for there is no other name under heaven given among men by which we must be saved" (Acts 4:12). One of the clearest statements of the purpose of Jesus' coming was "to seek and to save the lost" (Luke 19:10). Paul said that Jesus came to save sinners. Paul also said that he was the foremost or chief sinner (1 Tim. 1:16). This purpose for the coming of Christ into the world is basic and will be assumed throughout this book.

Some Christians, however, neglect the historic Jesus and the life He lived. They tend to forget—or at least they do not emphasize as much as they should—such Scriptures as, "The Word became flesh and dwelt among us, full of grace and truth; we have beheld his glory, glory as of the only Son from the Father" (John 1:14). Some also tend to overlook many other Scriptures, such as Paul's statement in Philippians:

> Have this mind among yourselves, which is yours in Christ Jesus, who, though he was in the form of God, did not count equality with God a thing to be grasped, but emp-

tied himself, taking the form of a servant, being born in the likeness of men. And being found in human form he humbled himself and became obedient unto death, even death on a cross (Phil. 2:5-8).

Many fail to give proper attention to the life that Jesus lived while He walked among people. This area, as is true of many aspects of the Christian life, should be both/and rather than either/or: Christ was both human and divine. He was and is deeply concerned about our salvation, but He was and is deeply concerned about the kinds of lives we live. Will you not agree that those of us who are conservative in our theology should give more attention to the kind of life He lived and the kind of life He wants us to live for Him?

What has just been said should not be interpreted as suggesting that our theology is of little importance. What we believe concerning the Bible, God, Christ, people, sin, and salvation is tremendously important. I will seek to emphasize in this book that equally important is the kind of lives we live, including the spirit we manifest toward those with whom we may disagree theologically. After all, the lives we live are more convincing to the rank and file of people, Christians and non-Christians alike, than our position on any theological matter. We are saved by grace through faith (Eph. 2:8), but we should not forget that "faith by itself, if it has no works, is dead. But some one will say, 'You have faith and I have works.' Show me your faith apart from your works, and I by my works will show you my faith. . . . For as the body apart from the spirit is dead, so faith apart from works is dead" (Jas. 2:17-18,26). Some of us may need to rediscover the Book of James and recognize that it is part of the inspired Word of God.

This book is an attempt to reexamine the kind of life

Jesus lived during His earthly journey. I hope that you and I will let the life He lived speak to us. If we do, most of us will discover that we fall far short of being what we ought to be for Him. Also, we may discover that we and our churches are tending to neglect some of the people for whom Jesus evidently had a special concern.

The idea for this particular book came to me about four o'clock one morning when I was awake and could not go back to sleep. The ideas for several of the chapters were formulated before I arose the next morning. This whole project has gripped me as nothing else for a long while.

Let me share with you some verses of Scripture which have challenged me for many years. "By this we may be sure that we are in him: he who says he abides in him ought to walk in the same way in which he walked" (1 John 2:5-6). The word for "walk" is *peripateō* which literally means "walk around"; it is a metaphor for *live* and is so translated in some contemporary versions.

The ministry of Jesus was primarily a walking ministry. He was a walking or a peripatetic teacher. What did He do as He walked? "He went about doing good" (Acts 10:38). Every great moral and religious teacher teaches as much if not more by what he does than by what he says. We should never forget, Jesus was the greatest teacher who ever lived. One source or proof of His greatness was the fact that He exemplified fully or perfectly in His own life all that He taught.

The chapters in this book will seek to spell out to some degree the kind of life Jesus lived as He walked among people. The major recurring question for us is, How much do we walk as He walked? If we are Christians, we claim to abide in Him; we should seek to live as He lived.

I hope you will read and study these chapters with an

open, searching mind and spirit. May the good Lord bless and in turn make you a blessing as you touch the lives of others.

T. B. MASTON

The following commentaries that follow
a verse-by-verse format are abbreviated
within the body of this book as follows:

Bar.—Barclay

Cam. B.—Cambridge Bible

Ell.—Ellicott's Commentary on the
Whole Bible

Exp. G.—Expositor's Greek Testament

W. P.—Word Pictures in the New
Testament

CONTENTS

To Walk as He Walked

1
Introduction

Two verses of Scripture somewhat summarize what Jesus did while He lived in the world. One verse comes at the close of the striking and fruitful visit Jesus had in the home of Zacchaeus. After Zacchaeus had given evidence of being a new creature in Christ, Jesus said, "For the Son of man came to seek and to save the lost" (Luke 19:10). Paul said, "The saying is sure and worthy of full acceptance, that Christ Jesus came into the world to save sinners. And I am the foremost of sinners" (1 Tim. 1:15).

The other verse, along with Luke 19:10, which fairly well summarizes the kind of life Jesus lived while He was among us is a part of Peter's message in the house of Cornelius. In that message, Peter said, "God anointed Jesus of Nazareth with the Holy Spirit and with power; how he went about doing good and healing all that were oppressed by the devil, for God was with him" (Acts 10:38). After this introductory chapter, each succeeding chapter of this book will center on some aspect of the ministry of Jesus that underscores the fact that He went about doing good and also will suggest that Jesus' followers should likewise go about doing good.

Announcement of His Messiahship

We should be deeply grateful for the way the Synoptic Gospels supplement one another. Luke was the only one who recorded the occasion when Jesus formally announced that He was the promised Messiah. Jesus also at that time set forth some of the characteristics that would be evidence of His messiahship (Luke 4:16-30). He did this at Nazareth "where he had been brought up" (v. 16). Can you imagine the setting? He went to the synagogue "as his custom was, . . . he stood up to read; and there was given to him the book [scroll, NEB, NIV] of the prophet Isaiah." Can you visualize Him turning the scroll until He found the section assigned for that day or possibly the verses He personally chose to read?

The verses were 61:1-2 and some words from Isaiah 58:6 ("to let the oppressed go free"), which he doubtlessly turned back to and read. The verses describe the coming Messiah. (You might like to turn to Isaiah 58 and read verses 6 and 7. It could be that Jesus actually read more than Luke recorded. Even if He did not, it is possible that many who heard Him that day knew the content and emphasis of the verses.)

After standing to read, Jesus sat down to speak or preach, which was the custom of that day. It was doubtlessly the first time he had spoken or preached in the presence of neighbors who had known Him and His family. His first words were: "Today this scripture has been fulfilled in your hearing" (v. 21). What a challenging statement!

Jesus had been ministering and preaching elsewhere. He had already developed a considerable reputation as a teacher. But He evidently wanted to delay the announcement that He was the promised Messiah until He was in the place "where he had been brought up" (v. 16). Those who heard Him that day had known Him as the son of the carpenter. His mother, brothers, and sisters were neighbors of theirs. Now, He came back claiming to be the promised Messiah. No wonder when He sat in the place for a speaker or preacher that "the eyes of all in the synagogue were fixed on him" (v. 20). Then Jesus plainly and pointedly stated, "Today this scripture has been fulfilled in your hearing" (v. 21).

Our interest in this incident from Jesus' life is not primarily regarding the reaction to His message. Rather, our interest is in the Scripture read that describes the kind of Messiah He was to be:

> The Spirit of the Lord is upon me,
> because he has anointed me to preach good
>   news to the poor.
> He has sent me to proclaim release to the
>   captives
> and recovering of sight to the blind,
> to set at liberty those who are oppressed,
> to proclaim the acceptable year of the Lord
>   (Luke 4:18-19).

"The acceptable year of the Lord" evidently referred to the year of Jubilee when mortgaged land was returned to its owner, slaves were freed, and debts were canceled. It can be implied that Jesus was saying that He, as the promised Messiah, would bring in "the acceptable year of the Lord." The year of Jubilee when there would be a restructuring of all of life. The main thrust, however, of the words from Isaiah was that the major emphasis in the ministry of the Messiah was to be to the oppressed, the underprivileged in general. Christ's mission was to a wounded world; his mission centered among the poor and outcasts of society.

Some disciples of John the Baptist reported to him on one occasion about the teachings and miracles of Jesus. John, from prison, sent two of his disciples to ask Jesus, "Are you he who is to come, or shall we look for another?" (Luke 7:19). While these disciples were with Jesus, He healed many people. He told them to return to John and tell him what they had seen and heard. Then, possibly after a pause for emphasis, He added, "The poor have good news preached to them" (v. 22). John knew his Old Testament. My judgment is that, when they mentioned the preaching of the gospel or good news to the poor, John's mind went back to Isaiah 61:2. John said within himself, *If that is what He is doing, then He is the Messiah.*

Now, a simple but pointed question: How much of a place do contemporary Christians and churches have for a ministry to and for the poor and underprivileged in general? Do we exert as much energy in reaching the poor as we do the well-to-do in our community? Are we primarily interested in reaching those who can contribute something to our churches or in reaching those to whom our church can make a contribution? Do we have effective programs to minister to and meet the needs of the poor, the people who hurt, the underprivileged? Senator Mark Hatfield says, "The great challenge of the Christian church today: to go out and identify with human need."

A Recurring Invitation

One day early in His public ministry, Jesus was walking along the shore of the Sea of Galilee. "He saw two brothers, Simon who is called Peter and Andrew his brother, casting a net into the sea; for they were fishermen. And he said to them, 'Follow me, and I will make you fishers of men.' Immediately they left their nets and followed him" (Matt. 4:18-19). Continuing around the shore, He also saw James and John in a boat with their father. Jesus gave James and John a similar invitation, and they immediately responded (v. 22).

These sets of brothers had met Jesus previously. John the Baptist had pointed him out to two of his followers or disciples and said, "Behold, the Lamb of God!" (John 1:36). We know that one of those was Andrew, and it is generally agreed that the other was John, the writer of the Fourth Gospel. The record says that Andrew "first found his brother Simon, and said to him, 'We have found the Messiah' " (v. 41). And so far as we know, the first word of Jesus to Simon was, "'So you are Simon the son of John? You shall be called Cephas' (which means Peter)" (v. 24).

Since that time, Jesus has continued to change those who are brought or come to Him. He will take whatever skills and training you and I may have and use them; He will also increase them. We will find our maximum fulfillment as we respond to Jesus' invitation to follow Him. It costs something to follow Jesus, but it also "pays to serve Jesus, it pays every day, it pays every step of the way," according to the hymnist.

Furthermore, as implied, if we will follow Him, Jesus will make us something we are not. But we should never forget that we must respond to His invitation: "Come, follow me." We should always remember He will never ask us to go anywhere He has not gone or ask us to do anything He has not done or will not do. Also, as someone has suggested, the resurrected Christ still has two hands—one to point the way He would have us go and the other to help us along that way.

Jesus' initial invitation was a recurring one which was

spelled out specifically at different times in His ministry. The same will be true in our experience with Jesus. His initial invitation to us came when we opened our lives and let Him come in. His word then was, "Follow me." As we have sought to follow Him, we have heard from time to time additional invitations to follow Him. In essence, His word to each of His followers is, "Your response to my initial call or invitation will be followed by additional insights and new ways into which you are to enter." In other words, the invitation to follow Him is a recurring invitation. The best assurance that we will know the way in which He wants us to walk tomorrow is to be responsive to His leading today.

Let us now look at specific places in the Scriptures where it is clearly revealed that the invitation to follow Him was and continues to be a recurring experience. One of the most striking examples is the incident of the rich young ruler. We have to read both Matthew's and Luke's records of the incident to know that he was a young ruler —Luke simply says "a ruler" (18:18) while Matthew refers to him as a "young man" (19:20). Mark simply refers to him as "a man" (10:17).

The young ruler asked Jesus what he needed to do to inherit eternal life. Jesus quoted the Ten Commandments which deal with right relations to one's fellowmen and then added, "You shall love your neighbor as yourself," which is from Leviticus 19:18 (Matt. 19:18-19). If we loved our neighbors as ourselves, we would keep the so-called second table of the Law. Did the young man notice that Jesus did not quote one of the Ten Commandments related to one's responsibility to one's neighbor? If Jesus had quoted, "You shall not covet" (Ex. 20:17), could the rich young ruler have responded honestly: "All these I have observed" (Matt. 19:20)? The Synoptic Gospels record the invitation of Jesus to the young man, "Come, follow me" (Matt. 19:21; Mark 10:21; Luke 18:22).

At Caesarea Philippi, Jesus gave the disciples an examination to see how well they understood the kind of Messiah He had come to be. This was about six months before his crucifixion and resurrection. He asked them, "Who do men say that the Son of man is?" (Matt. 16:13). They gave various answers. Then He asked them the pointed question, "But who do you say that I am?" (v. 15). Typically, Peter spoke up and said, "You are the Christ, the Son of the living God" (v. 16). This is the background for the statement that Jesus began to reveal to His disciples that crucifixion and resurrection awaited Him in Jerusalem. How grateful we should be that He never mentioned His crucifixion without at the same time mentioning His resurrection. It has been suggested that the two events are so closely interrelated that they should always be referred to together as "crucifixion-resurrection."

From that background, Jesus said to the disciples, "If any man would come after me, let him deny himself and take up his cross and follow me" (v. 24). Again, we should be grateful that He added, "For whoever would save his life will lose it, and whoever loses his life for my sake will find it" (v. 25). In other words, in the Christian life, there is no real crucifixion without resurrection and no resurrection without crucifixion. Also, the implication of Jesus' statement is that for His disciples, then and now, to follow Him means or necessitates the crucifixion of self with selfish purposes and ambitions. But how glorious to remember that as followers of His deny self, they discover self on the highest level. In other words, crucifixion is followed by resurrection.

This section would not be complete without the addition of at least one other invitation. This invitation may not be directly related to the main thrust of this book. But it was an invitation by Jesus that has come to followers through the centuries. Many of us can testify it has been a recurring, repeated invitation to us ever since we were introduced to Jesus. Some of us do not know what we would have done at times if we had not been touched anew by the wonderful words of that invitation with its assurance: "Come to me, all who labor and are heavy laden, and I will give you rest" (Matt. 11:28). This invitation is not complete, however, without the inclusion of the two succeeding verses: "Take my yoke upon you, and learn from me; for I am gentle and lowly in heart, and you will find rest for your souls. For my yoke is easy, and my burden is light" (vv. 29-30).

The last two verses, on the surface, may sound contradictory to the invitation with its promise. On the surface, there even seems to be a contradiction in verses 29-30. A yoke is a burden. How can we find rest and relief from the pressures and burdens of life by taking up a yoke? The seeming conflict is relieved, however, by the consciousness that Jesus, our Lord and Savior, is under the yoke with us. His burden can and does become light as we are conscious of the fact that He is under the load or burden with us.

A Closing Exhortation

Many of you have had the experience of a verse or a passage of Scripture suddenly becoming alive for you. You may have read it many times previously, but suddenly it gripped you as it never had before. I have had a few such experiences, one of which I want to share with you. I can visualize clearly where I was when the verse first gripped me. I was seated on the platform of the institution where I taught. There was a special student meeting on the campus. The speaker referred to or quoted a verse that grabbed me and has continued to challenge me through the years.

On resurrection day, Jesus had appeared to Mary Magdalene; she, in turn, reported to His disciples. "On the evening of that day" (John 20:19), Jesus appeared to the disciples and said to them, "Peace be with you," which was a form of greeting. It would be interesting to know what all they had talked about, but we do know that He said to them, "As the Father has sent me, even so I send you" (v. 21). These are the words that gripped me and have continued to challenge me. I asked then and have continued to ask, What did Jesus mean? I have come to at least some tentative conclusions which I think are applicable to us as Jesus' contemporary followers.

The initial invitation of Jesus was and still is, "Come, follow me." Jesus' closing exhortation was, "So I send you." The initial and recurring invitation to follow was and is, to a considerable degree, preparatory. One test of whether we have heard and responded to His invitation, "Come, follow me," is whether we have heard and heeded His exhortation or command to go. How clearly have you and I heard and how readily have we responded to His words, "So I send you"? The way we honestly answer that question will largely determine the effectiveness of our lives for Him and His cause.

Too much space would be needed to spell out in detail the nature of Jesus' conviction that He had been sent by the Father. There is no doubt that He had a deep sense of having been sent. He said to the disciples, "My food is to do the will of him who sent me, and to accomplish his work" (John 4:34). We, Jesus' disciples, should have a sense of having been sent. How grateful we should be that we do not have to go alone, since the resurrected Christ promised, "Lo, I am with you always, to the close of the age" (Matt. 28:20).

The deep sense of having been sent gave Jesus a sense of holy urgency. On one occasion, He said to the disciples, "We must work the works of him who sent me, while it is day; night comes, when no one can work" (John 9:4). A sense of having been sent by Him will give to each of us a sense of holy urgency.

The other chapters of this book will seek to spell out, to some degree, what Jesus was sent to do and what we should be doing for Him.

A statement by the resurrected Christ to the disciples should encourage us: "When he had said this, he breathed on them, and said to them, 'Receive the Holy Spirit'" (John 20:22). We are or should be sent ones; and thank the Lord, we have Someone to go with us!

The next chapter will attempt to set forth, in an admittedly incomplete manner, the fact that Jesus revealed God. That was one purpose of Jesus' coming into the world. The other chapters will seek to set forth some aspects of the life He lived that revealed the Father and hence revealed what He was sent into the world to do. We will concentrate on the aspects of Jesus' life that underscore the fact that He went about doing good. You will recognize there are some aspects of the kind of life Jesus lived that could not be set forth in detail because of lack of space. An attempt will be made to major on those phases of His life that seem to be most needed by contemporary Christians and churches.

Let us as individual children of God never forget that we are sent ones; we are on a mission for the Lord. Such a sense of mission should be true for every child of God regardless of his or her vocation or calling. What a revolution it would mean in contemporary churches if this were a reality and not merely an ideal. Again, let me make it personal: How much of a conviction do you and I have that we are sent ones, sent by the resurrected Christ who lives within us and seeks to express Himself through us in the home, the church, the community, and in all our interpersonal relationships?

Summary Statements

Some of these summary statements could just as properly be considered "introductory statements" and could have been the first section of this chapter or in the preface.

① Throughout the stream of Christian history, believers have, from time to time, tended to neglect either the Deity or the humanity of Christ.

② In the contemporary period, conservative Protestants in general are tending to neglect Jesus' human nature. Hence, they fail to give enough attention to the kind of life He lived while He walked among people. We need to keep in proper balance the fact that He was the Son of God and our Savior and the fact that He was also the son of Mary and our Older Brother. As our Older Brother, He "has been tempted as we are," but we are grateful for the additional words, "yet without sin" (Heb. 4:15). This is the basis for our assurance that He understands when we are tempted. Also, "yet without sin" gives us the assurance of a source for victory in times of temptation.

③ As a result of the contemporary tendency of conservative Christians to neglect the human nature of Jesus, too many stress "orthodoxy of belief " without a comparable emphasis on "orthodoxy of life." It is tragic, but some even tend to substitute the former for the latter. In other words, some make orthodoxy of belief a substitute for real Christian living. Do not misunderstand: What one be-

lieves about God, people, sin, salvation, and many other
truths is most important. The emphasis I am seeking to
make, and will seek to make in the chapters of this book,
is that the kind of life one lives for Christ and others is a
valid and necessary revelation of what one believes.

4. It may be wise for all of us to remember that Jesus
Himself said: "Not everyone who says to me, 'Lord, Lord,'
shall enter the kingdom of heaven, but he who does the
will of my Father who is in heaven" (Matt. 7:21). (Read
verses 22-23 if you do not remember their content.)

5. Regarding the time when "the Son of man comes in
his glory," Jesus revealed that there would be the great
separation of the sheep and the goats (Matt. 25:31-46).
This is a passage of Scripture that we will come back to in
a later chapter, but one particular emphasis is applicable
to our immediate concern. What would be the basis of the
separation? While what we believe, as previously suggested, is important, the basis for the separation would be
what they had done and particularly their treatment of
the underprivileged—the people who hurt: the hungry,
the thirsty, the stranger, the naked, the sick, the impris-
oned. Note that the King identified with those who hurt
(vv. 40-45). Will you not agree that many, possibly most,
of our churches tend to neglect the very persons with
whom Jesus identified?

As suggested previously, the preceding is not meant to
minimize what we believe. It simply underscores the fact
that the proof of what we believe is in the lives we live.
It underscores what James so plainly wrote, "Faith apart
from works is dead" (Jas. 2:26; see 2:17).

6. Our discussion of the Christian life should not be, in
most cases, an either/or but a both/and discussion. We
need a balancing of emphasis on the divine and the
human nature of Jesus: the fact that He was and is the Son

of God but also the son of Mary. We need also a balancing of emphasis on orthodoxy of belief and orthodoxy of life, "orthopraxy."

⑦ Jesus is the world's greatest teacher. One thing that underscores Jesus' greatness as a teacher was the fact that He exemplified in His life what He taught. And, after all, effective moral and religious teachers teach as much if not more by the lives they live than by anything they specifically say or teach.

Challenging Quotations

The following are some quotations and adaptations that can and should challenge you and me. I hope that you will meditate on them and critically evaluate each of them.
Athanasius:

> Christ does not heal us by standing over and against us, diagnosing our sickness, prescribing medicine for us to take, and then going away, to leave us to get better by obeying his instructions—as an ordinary doctor might. No. He becomes the patient! He assumes that very humanity which is in need of redemption, and by being anointed by the Spirit in our humanity by a life of perfect obedience, by dying and rising again, for us, our humanity is healed *in him.* We are not just healed "through Christ" because of the work of Christ, but "in and through Christ."

Irenaeus: "He [Jesus] became what we are . . . in order that He might make us as He Himself is." But we must cooperate with Him in the making process. The more fully we respond to Him, the more like Him we will become.

Senator Mark Hatfield: "Surely the Christ who befriended the Samaritan woman at the well, who cared for the sick, who fed the hungry, and who blessed children—

surely this Christ has something to say to us today." Will you agree that what he says is needed by many of us as children of God and by many and possibly most of our churches?

C. R. Daley, Jr., in an editorial said, "Genuine spiritual regeneration is validated by holy living, and where there is no holy living, there's been no holy transaction."

David Moberg said, "Even while claiming not to be conformed to this world, evangelicals are subtly squeezed into its mold (Rom. 12:1-2). Such sinful conformity is especially great in regard to Christian social responsibility."

Now, let us turn to some quotations from the eighth-century prophets. Isaiah, the prince of the prophets, after he had painted a dark picture of the judgment of the Lord on the children of Israel because of their sins, added:

> Wash yourselves; make yourselves clean;
>   remove the evil of your doings
>   from before my eyes;
> cease to do evil,
>   learn to do good;
> seek justice,
>   correct oppression;
> defend the fatherless,
>   plead for the widow (Isa. 1:16-17).

Amos, speaking for the Lord, said:

> For I know how many are your transgressions,
>   and how great are your sins—
> you who afflict the righteous, who take a bribe,
>   and turn aside the needy in the gate (Amos 5:12).

Again, Amos said:

> Hear this, you who trample upon the needy,
>   and bring the poor of the land to an end,

saying, "When will the new moon be over,

....

that we may buy the poor for silver
and the needy for a pair of sandals"
(Amos 8:4-6).

Let us never forget that the powerful eighth-century prophets were defenders of the poor and under-privileged. Also, Jesus revealed a special concern for the underprivileged in general. Do we follow in Jesus' and the prophets' train?

What do you think might happen if you and I attempted to live in harmony with the teachings of the Old Testament prophets and to walk or live as Jesus walked or lived?

A couple of verses in 1 John came alive for me a few years ago. I was sitting with my family in our accustomed place in our church for the morning worship service. I do not remember what the pastor preached on or anything about the service except a Scripture the pastor quoted or read. I had read it before, but it suddenly came alive and has challenged me since that time as no other passage of Scripture. I have used it many times in speaking to young people, but it is equally applicable to older Christians. I have said on numerous occasions, "If you will let these words really grip you, they will challenge you to the end of life's journey." These words, along with the verse where Peter said that Jesus "went about doing good," have provided most of the inspiration and background for the chapters of this book.

The words from 1 John are:

By this we may be sure that we are in him: he who says

*he abides in him ought to walk in the same way in which
he walked* (2:5-6, author's italics)

We say that we abide in Him when we claim to be
Christians. The word for "walk" can be and is sometimes
translated "live." "Ought" is a business term and means
that we are obligated or in debt. What a challenge to
every child of God, young or old! We will never walk or
live perfectly or fully as Jesus walked or lived, but are we
seeking to and are we making progress in that way?

Note

1. David O. Moberg, *The Great Reversal: Evangelism and
Social Concern* (Philadelphia: J. B. Lippincott Co., 1972), p. 36.

2
He Revealed God

Jesus, while He dwelt among people, did nothing more important than what He revealed concerning God. My theology teacher of many years ago said that Jesus, when He came into the world, had basically a twofold mission: to reveal God and to redeem people. He also stated that these two purposes were so closely related that he was not sure which should be first.

One truth revealed about God by Jesus and in the Scriptures in general is the fact that God is three in one: Father, Son, and Holy Spirit. This is extremely difficult for many, and possibly most, Christians to comprehend.

We can understand, at least to a limited degree, how they can be one in nature, spirit, and will. But how can they be considered one? The nearest we have such in human relations is identical twins. Some identical twins not only look much alike but some look so much alike that people cannot distinguish between them. Also, some identical twins think largely alike, have strikingly similar ambitions, emotions, tastes, and the like. There may be a husband and wife who have lived many years together and have become so well adapted to each other that toward the end of life's journey they have become one to an unusual degree. It should be recognized, however, that no human relationship is or can be entirely comparable to

the relationship of the Father, Son, and Holy Spirit. As
children of God, we can and do accept by faith what we
cannot understand fully.

How did Jesus reveal God as He went about doing
good? Basically, He revealed God by what He said or
taught about God and by the kind of life He lived. What
did Jesus reveal concerning God in His teachings and in
His life?

The God revealed by Jesus is somewhat different from
the God known by people in general at that time. God had
sought to reveal Himself to men and women through the
ages, but they could not fully comprehend that revelation. That was one of the purposes for which Jesus, the
Son, came into the world. However, even with Jesus' coming, many of us who know Him cannot completely grasp
the revelation of God.

The Nature of God

Several principles Jesus taught concerning God are of
real importance to people in general and to Christians in
particular. After all, we as children of God will prove our
kinship to Him as our Heavenly Father by building into
our lives some of the character traits found in Him. It is
true that no one except Jesus has fully and perfectly revealed the Father. However, the fact that we do not and
cannot express perfectly the character and nature of God
should not and must not keep us from making an effort to
do so. We should measure our lives by nothing less than
the perfect revelation of the Father by His only Son, our
Lord and Savior.

The consciousness of how far we fall short should give
to us a deep sense of our sin coupled with a genuine
humility. But our failure to measure up fully should never
be permitted to defeat us. Rather, it should be a constant

challenge to come up higher, to strive harder, and to depend more on the indwelling Spirit to give us the determination and grace we need to live more and more like the One who lives in us and seeks to express Himself through us.

In order to live more like Jesus lived and to worship properly, we need to understand the nature of God. In the course of the conversation with the Samaritan woman at the well, Jesus pointedly said, "God is spirit, and those who worship him must worship in spirit and truth" (John 4:24). Since God is spirit, the worship of Him is not and cannot be restricted to a particular locale. If your experiences have been similar to mine, and those of many of my friends, some of the most meaningful worship experiences have been outdoors around a campfire, at a sunrise or a sunset service, or sitting alone in meditation. It is true, however, that most who have felt the touch of the divine Spirit in a congenial group or alone outside are those who are most responsive to a well-planned worship service in their churches. God is spirit and we, His children, must be responsive to the touch of His Spirit if we have a genuine experience of worship anywhere.

We know that God is spirit and is to be worshiped in spirit and truth. Now what are some of the general character traits of God mentioned by Jesus? In the monumental sixth chapter of Matthew—a portion of the Sermon on the Mount—Jesus suggested that God is the One who knows: "Your Father knows what you need before you ask" (v. 8). He forgives: "If you forgive men their trespasses, your heavenly Father also will forgive you" (Matt. 6:14). He also rewards: "Your Father who sees in secret will reward you" (Matt. 6:18).

When Jesus talked about the shepherd and the sheep, He mentioned the tremendous truth that the Father who

had given Him the sheep "is greater than all, and no one
is able to snatch them out of the Father's hand." Then He
closed this statement with those wonderful words, "I and
the Father are one" (John 10:29-30). What a great assurance this should give us. If we are Christians, we are in the
hands of Jesus; His hand is in the Father's hand. No one
can break that grip!

A wonderful statement in Hebrews goes: "In many and
various ways [in fragmentary and varied fashion, NEB]
God spoke of old to our fathers by the prophets; but in
these last days he has spoken to us by a Son, . . . He reflects
the glory of God and bears the very stamp of his nature
[exact representation of His nature, NASB]" (1:1-3). Once
Philip said to Jesus, " 'Lord, show us the Father, and we
shall be satisfied.' Jesus said to him, . . . 'He who has seen
me has seen the Father' " (John 14:8-9). Why not read the
entire fourteenth chapter of John, or at least verses 8-11
that record the conversation Jesus had with Thomas and
Philip, meditate on it, and let it warm your heart?

John, who possibly understood Jesus better than any of
the other apostles, declared that God works (John 5:17), is
light (1 John 1:5), and is love (1 John 4:8,16).

Jesus revealed God more by the life He lived than by
anything He ever spoke about God. The greatness of Jesus
as a teacher was deepened by the fact that He exemplified
in His life everything that He taught.

Who are some of the greatest Christians you have
known? We know about some: David Livingstone of
Africa; Frank Laubach, who taught so many underprivileged people of the world to read; Kagawa, the Japa-
nese Christian of a couple of generations ago who gave
himself so unselfishly to the neglected masses of Japan;
and Mother Teresa, of our day, whose work among the

diseased, poor masses was recognized with the Nobel Peace Prize.

I wonder, however, if your experience has been similar to mine. Some of the best Christians I have known through the years have been among God's little people. These people have never been widely recognized for anything they have accomplished. However, they are men, women, and youth of real integrity. They exemplify quietly and unpretentiously the spirit of Jesus.

The Power of God

Some phases of God's power are clearly demonstrated in the Old Testament. Victory or defeat was frequently attributed to the intervention of God or His failure to intervene. The children of Israel were given the encouraging word: "The Lord your God is he that goes with you, . . . to give you the victory" (Deut. 20:4). That promise was given consistently to the children of Israel. Jonathan, in pleading with his father for David, mentioned that David "took his life in his hand and he slew the Philistine." Notice what follows: "And the Lord wrought a great victory for all Israel" (1 Sam. 19:5).

Samuel said that the Lord gave victory to David wherever he went (2 Sam. 8:6,14). A great victory is attributed to the Lord in 2 Sam. 23:10,12. The psalmist said:

> All the ends of the earth have seen
> the victory of our God (Ps. 98:3).

The wise man said:

> The horse is made ready for the day of battle,
> but the victory belongs to the Lord
> (Prov. 21:31).

Over and over again throughout the Old Testament, victory is attributed to the power of God (Zech. 12:7).

The concept of the power of God revealed in the life and teachings of Jesus goes beyond and is a fulfillment of the concept of the power of God frequently mentioned and demonstrated in the Old Testament. In the latter, God's power was primarily seen as power to defeat the enemies of His people. This meant at times their destruction. But the fuller revelation of God recorded in the New Testament, the power of God revealed and demonstrated by Jesus, was primarily power to control what He had created. It was a power that was used to bless and heal rather than to destroy. This was even true of the enemies of God's people and His own enemies.

As Jesus went about doing good, He from time to time revealed the power of God to control what He had created and to heal. One striking example of God's power to control what He had created was the stilling of the storm on the Sea of Galilee. Jesus and the disciples were crossing the sea after what had evidently been a tiring day. Jesus, revealing His human nature, was tired and was asleep in the boat. He did not wake even though "a great storm of wind arose, and the waves beat into the boat, so that the boat was already filling" (Mark 4:37). The disciples woke Jesus and said, "Teacher, do you not care if we perish?" (v. 38).

The other Synoptic Gospels record the incident. When they woke Jesus, Matthew and Luke simply record a statement. Mark alone has the question, "Teacher, do you not care if we perish?" It is rather generally agreed that Mark received considerable material for his Gospel from Peter. Could it be that Peter was the one who asked the question?

The main thought, however, from our perspective, is

the fact that where there had been "a great storm" Jesus arose and spoke to the wind and there "was a great calm" (v. 39). The pointed questions of Jesus were, "Why are you afraid? Have you no faith?" (v. 40). No wonder they said to one another, "Who then is this, that even wind and sea obey him?" (v. 41). Most of us will never be on a lake in a storm with Jesus, but there are other storms of life that are and may be equally destructive. We can be sure when these storms arise that if we are children of God He will be in the boat with us. We can be equally sure that if we will trust Him He will reveal again the power of our Heavenly Father to quiet the storms that may threaten us.

The miracles of healing also underscored the power of God to control that which He created. A brief look at two of those miracles must suffice. Jairus, "a ruler of the synagogue," had an "only daughter" who was about twelve years of age. She was dying (Luke 8:42; see Matt. 9:18; Mark 5:23). Jairus asked Jesus to go to his house and heal his daughter. While they were on the way, a man from Jairus's house met them and said that the girl was dead and that he should not bother the Master any more.

But Jesus, who revealed fully the compassion and power of the Father, said, "Only believe, and she shall be well" (v. 50). Taking only the father and mother of the twelve-year-old and Peter, John, and James, Jesus entered the room where the child's body lay. We have to keep alert to the little things in the life of Jesus to judge His tenderness. Can you visualize Him taking the girl by the hand and, I think in a very tender tone, saying, "Child arise"? Another evidence of His tenderness is that He directed that something be given her to eat. No wonder "her parents were amazed" (Luke 8:40-42,49-56). Jesus revealed not only the power of God but also His concern and compassion for people who were in need. God's power is never simply revealed to prove His power. It was, and still is, used to minister to people in need.

One other miracle of Jesus that reveals and proves the power of God will be mentioned. It is the raising of Lazarus, the good friend of Jesus. Why not read again prayerfully and meditatively John 11? You might even like to read the first eight verses of chapter 12.

Jesus had deliberately delayed His return to Bethany, the home of Lazarus, Martha, and Mary. When He and the disciples arrived, Lazarus had been dead four days. But the Father, who is the source of life, can restore the life of one who is dead. This is one of several great truths revealed by this incident in the life of Jesus.

Several significant ideas can be pointed out concerning this whole incident. We assume that, as Martha suggested, if Jesus had been present He could have kept Lazarus from dying (v. 21). The Father who gives life can take it, but He can also restore it. And to Martha, Jesus made that great statement that has meant so much to so many through the years: "He who believes in me, though he die, yet shall he live, and whoever lives and believes in me shall never die" (vv. 25-26). In other words, when children of God are dead, they, in reality, are alive. And they are alive in a sense and to a degree that they have never known.

The whole incident also reveals the balancing of the power and the tenderness of God. When Jesus saw Mary weeping as she came to meet Him and "the Jews who came with her also weeping, he was deeply moved in spirit and troubled" (v. 33). That is the background for the shortest verse in the Bible: "Jesus wept." That verse reveals much about Jesus and the Father He revealed. There is no necessary conflict between power and compassion. The former can be dangerous unless it is balanced and controlled by compassion and tenderness.

As Father

We have seen the power of God revealed by Jesus. God's power to control what He has created is revealed in a particular way in His miracles. Most of the miracles of Jesus were performed to relieve some human need. They revealed our Heavenly Father's concern and compassion for people who hurt. Jesus, who fully revealed the Father, seemed inevitably to respond when He came into contact with a person whose body was broken, whose mind was demented, or who had some heavy burden to carry.

One verse, the "little gospel," summarizes the Father's attitude toward suffering humanity, including you and me: "For God so loved the world that he gave his only Son, that whosoever believes in him should not perish but have eternal life" (John 3:16). Paul, in his letter to the Romans, wrote, "But God shows his love for us in that while we were yet sinners Christ died for us" (5:8).

This One who died for us while we were yet sinners was and is the Son of God. No one concept of God is more central in the life and teachings of Jesus than that of fatherhood. The idea of God as Father is evident to some degree in the Old Testament (Deut. 32:6; Isa. 63:16; Jer. 3:19). It is central in the revelation of God by Jesus. The prevalence of "Father" applied to God is somewhat summarized in these statements from another book that I wrote.

In the New Testament there are approximately 275 references to God as Father, with over 100 of these in John's gospel and an additional dozen in 1 John. It is primarily

the Johannine writings that have made "Father" the more
or less natural name for God for Christians, although it is
used in the synoptic gospels and frequently in Paul's epistles.

One reason for the prevalence of "Father" as a name for
God in the New Testament is the fact that Jesus so frequently used the term. Many of the references of Jesus to
God as Father were simply to "the Father." Being conscious of a unique relation to God, he frequently referred
to God as "My Father." He also used the expression "your
Father," with nineteen such references in Matthew's gospel, with fifteen of them in the Sermon on the Mount and
all but four of them in chapter six.

It was in the Model Prayer that Jesus used the all-inclusive "Our Father." If God is "my Father" and "your Father," then he is "our Father." The word "our" of the
original prayer included Jesus and his disciples. Today it
includes all who have come into the family of God through
their union with the resurrected Christ.[1]

An additional statement from that book is one that all
of us should seek honestly to apply to our own lives. The
statement is as follows:

The "our Father" makes prayer drastically and for some
embarrassingly inclusive. . . . Can we pray "our Father"
with all of God's children: with those of other churches
and denominations, with those of other classes and castes,
with those of other colors and races? We should remember
that the God who is the father of all of his children cannot
really be "my Father" unless I can accept him as "your
Father" and hence as "our Father."[2]

Although God, in the deepest sense, is the Father only
of those who have come into His spiritual family through
their faith in the Son, God expresses His fatherly attitude
toward all people. Jesus said that our Heavenly Father

makes His sun to rise "on the evil and on the good, and sends rain on the just and on the unjust" (Matt. 5:45). This means that our God has a fatherly attitude even toward those who do not acknowledge Him as their Father. We who are children of God should have a brotherly attitude toward all people, even those who are not our spiritual brothers and sisters.

Jesus also plainly said that, since God is our Father and knows our needs, we should not worry or be anxious about what we shall eat, drink, or wear. We, His children, should seek first His kingdom and His righteousness with the calm assurance that our Father will provide for us the necessities of life.

Still another glorious concept about God, our Heavenly Father, is that He knows His children by name. We are not a mass of unknowns. We know from the Scriptures that God called some individuals by name: Moses (Ex. 3:4), Samuel (1 Sam. 3:4), Elijah (1 Kings 19:9,13). Some people may contend that these were some of God's great leaders. But knowing our Heavenly Father as we know Him in Christ, we believe that He is impartial in His treatment of His children. He has no "great ones" except those who are great in service. And God's great servants are not restricted to any class of people. Some of the humblest are among His greatest.

But whatever our status in the work of our God in the world, we believe He individualizes us—He knows us by name. Jesus, referring to Himself as the shepherd, said that as Shepherd He knows His sheep by name. He also said that the sheep recognize His voice and follow Him (John 10:3-14).

In our family prayer, we correctly pray for individuals by name: members of our family, our friends, our fellow church members and church leaders, denominational leaders, our missionaries, and so forth. We have the assurance that our and their Heavenly Father knows them by name. Prayer for them by name makes our prayers more personal and meaningful. Thank You, Father, that You know us by name!

About God the Father, John Calvin said:

> Ever since God exhibited himself to us as a Father, we must be convicted of extreme ingratitude if we do not in turn exhibit ourselves as his sons. . . . Ever since he ingrafted us into his body, we, who are his members, should anxiously beware of contracting any stain or taint.[3]

Conclusion

Whatever may be your vocation or mine, our chief or supreme task, if we are Christians, is to reveal the Christ who fully revealed the Father, redeemed us, and is our Lord and Master. Kagawa once made a statement that I did not like when I first heard it. However, the more I thought about it, the more I was persuaded that he was right. He suggested that we as Christians should be "little Christs." In other words, he was suggesting that the biggest task and the deepest and dominant purpose of every child of God should be to live so those about us would see, at least to some degree, Christ living in us and expressing Himself through us. Do you agree?

We should recognize that many whose lives we touch will only know as much about our Lord and Savior as we reveal to them in the lives we live. Dare we ask the question and seek to answer it honestly: What kind of representative of Jesus are we to loved ones, neighbors, friends, and casual acquaintances? Possibly many of them never read the Bible except what they read in our lives. How accurate a translation are we of the kind of life Jesus lived while He lived on earth—the kind of life He still attempts to live in and through you and me? Do they read in us an accurate or a garbled translation?

> *By this we may be sure that we are in him: he who says he abides in him ought to walk in the same way in which he walked* (1 John 2:5-6, author's italics).

> *By this we know that we are in Him. He who says he abides in Him ought himself also to walk just as He walked* (1 John 2:5-6, NKJV, author's italics).

How much does the life we live reveal the Christ who lives within us and who fully revealed God, His Father and our Heavenly Father?

Notes

1. T. B. Maston, *Why Live the Christian Life?* (Nashville: Broadman Press, 1974), pp. 24-25.

2. Ibid.

3. John Calvin, *Institutes of Christian Religion*, II (Edinburgh: T. & T. Clark, n. d.), p. 4.

3
He Dignified Humanity

As Jesus went about doing good, He not only revealed God but also dignified humanity. To adapt a statement of Georgia Harkness, we see in the life of Christ what God was like and what people by the grace of God should become. The life he lived while He walked on earth is the kind of life Jesus' followers should live. This involves not only our relations to God but also to people. The challenge of living like or letting Christ express Himself through us will create in any serious child of God a constant stress or tension. However, there is no progress without such tension.

Dietrich Bonhoeffer suggested that "in Christ we are offered the possibility of partaking in the reality of God and in the reality of the world, but not in one without the other." A aspect of our participation in the life of the world is in our relation to members of our family and to people at large. Now, how did Jesus dignify humanity?

By His Human Nature

The twofold possibility spoken of by Bonhoeffer is grounded in and springs from the twofold nature of Jesus. Athanasius, an early Christian father, said that "Jesus was made man . . . that we might be made divine." Irenaeus, approximately a century before Athanasius, had said

49

something strikingly similar: "He became what we are
. . . in order that he could make us as he himself is."

Jesus is the Son of God but also the son of Mary. He is
the divine-human person. We mature as sons and daugh-
ters of our natural parents. We have the same potential
through union with Christ to mature as children of God.

Jesus evidently had a more or less normal childhood.
There were doubtlessly some things unique about Him as
a maturing child; but in general, He grew and matured as
did any other son or daughter. We know little about Jesus'
childhood. We do know that, in harmony with the custom
and law of the day, He was circumcised on the eighth day
(Luke 2:21). Upon going to the Temple for Mary's purifi-
cation, two of God's elderly believers in the Temple
recognized Him as a special child. We also know that His
mother "marveled at what was said about him" (Luke
2:33). About the only other fact we know about His early
childhood is that He "grew and became strong, filled with
wisdom; and the favor of God was upon Him" (Luke 2:40).

There is another brief glimpse into the life of Jesus
when He was twelve years of age. He tarried behind in
Jerusalem as His family and others were returning to their
home (Luke 2:41-49). When Joseph and Mary found Him
in the Temple "sitting among the teachers, listening to
them, and asking them questions; . . . they were astonished; and his mother said to him, 'Son, why have you
treated us so? Behold, your father and I have been looking
for you anxiously.' And he said to them, 'How is it that you
sought me? Did you not know that I must be in my Father's house? [about my Father's business, KVJ)]' " (vv.
46-49).

There is no way to find out how fully conscious Jesus was
at that time of His unique relation to the Heavenly Father. We do realize that He returned with His parents to

Nazareth and "was obedient to them" (v. 51)—also that "his mother kept all these things in her heart" (v. 51). She must have frequently reviewed in her mind the unusual things concerning her unique Son. There is the often-quoted summary statement: "Jesus increased in wisdom and in stature, and in favor with God and man" (v. 52; see also 1 Sam. 2:26).

There followed eighteen years of silence. The writers of the Gospels were not concerned primarily about those years. They picked up His life story when, in response to the will and purpose of the Father, He began His messianic mission. We know from what others said about Him that He evidently worked with Joseph at the carpenter's trade and that He had half brothers and sisters (Matt. 13:55-56; Mark 6:3). Also, we assume, in harmony with Jewish customs, that Jesus became the head of the family when Joseph died. We can be sure of one thing—every role He played, every function He performed, everything He did dignified His humanity and humanity in general. He set an example for every person in every area of life.

Some of us may have difficulty realizing that as the son of Mary, Jesus got tired, hungry, thirsty, and felt the need for human companionship. For example, "In Gethsemane he craved friendship. He prayed to God, but he reached out for Peter and John. The longing for friendship and the unrest of loneliness are proof of a truly human and social nature."[1]

There is no one thing that underscores Jesus' humanity more than the fact that He "in every respect has been tempted as we are" (Heb. 4:15). Comprehending how this could have been true of Jesus may be difficult for us. However, He would not have been fully human without being tempted. This is our assurance of an understanding Savior when we are tempted. How grateful we should be for the additional words: "yet without sinning." Because Jesus was tempted as we are and had the victory over temptations, we in confidence can "draw near to the throne of grace" and be assured that we will "find grace to help in time of need" (v. 16). In another place, the writer of Hebrews said, "For because he himself has suffered and been tempted, he is able to help those who are tempted" (Heb. 2:18). We are not able to live sinless lives, but in His strength we can increasingly have victory over the temptations that come.

By His Attitude Toward People

By Jesus' attitude toward and relation to people and particularly by His relation to the poor, the hungry, and people who hurt, Jesus dignified humanity. It should not be overlooked, however, that Jesus had a deep concern for and interest in all kinds of people—the privileged as well as the underprivileged. Some of His dearest and seemingly most helpful friends were not of the lower class. For example, evidently the Bethany home was not a home of poverty; no family was more appreciative of the presence of Jesus, and He felt closer to no other family than to Lazarus and his sisters, Martha and Mary. What a blessing it must have been to Jesus after a busy and doubtlessly at times a frustrating day in Jerusalem to have a quiet evening with His cherished friends.

Even within the inner circle of the disciples, among those who shared uniquely in His ministry, some would be considered middle or upper class today. Matthew was a tax collector. Tax collectors were not poverty stricken. Some others of the apostles were doubtlessly not poor. We are not sure how John was known by the high priest (John 18:16).

Although Jesus at times was extremely critical of the

Pharisees, He took time from a busy schedule to reason with Nicodemus, a Pharisee and a ruler of the Jews, about the new birth (John 3:1-13). We must not forget that Nicodemus, a Pharisee, and Joseph of Arimathea prepared the body of Jesus for burial and placed the body in the tomb (John 19:38-42). On at least three occasions, Jesus accepted the invitation to the home of a Pharisee (Luke 7:36-50; 11:37-41; 14:1-24). Jesus was and continues to be interested in reaching and ministering to all kinds of people.

The healing ministry of Jesus reached out to all classes. Several of Jesus' miracles were performed at the request of people from the middle and upper classes. Some examples are the nobleman's son (John 4:46-54); Jairus's daughter (Luke 8:40-42,49-56); the centurion's servant or slave (Luke 7:2-10; see Matt. 8:5-13); and the raising of Lazarus (John 11:1-44).

This section on the attitude toward and relation of Jesus to people would not have been complete without some reference to middle- or upper-class individuals or families. However, the attitude of Jesus toward people is much more vividly illustrated by His relation to the struggling masses, the poor, hungry, those who hurt, and the underprivileged. There is abundant evidence that He took the initiative in reaching out and ministering to their needs. These, in the main, were the very ones who from the perspective of the privileged did not and, too frequently, still do not have much dignity or worth. No one gets so low on the economic ladder or even on the moral ladder that Jesus would ignore or turn His back on him or her.

A striking illustration by Jesus found only in Luke's Gospel (16:19-31) is the story of Lazarus, a beggar, and a certain rich man "who was clothed in purple and fine linen and who feasted sumptuously every day." When the beggar died, he "was carried by the angels to Abraham's bosom." In contrast, the rich man, when he died, was in hell and in torment.

We should remember, however, that Jesus was not partial, but being impartial He inevitably gave more time and attention to the neglected masses than to any other group. In our day, if Jesus had to take sides, He would doubtlessly be on the side of the underprivileged. This would be true regardless of where they lived or the color of their skin. Jesus, in His deep concern for and interest in all kinds of people but His seeming partiality to the underprivileged, relates very closely to the Old Testament prophets, particularly to the great eighth-century prophets—Isaiah, Micah, Amos, and Hosea.

The poor, hungry, and underprivileged were not only the neglected ones of His day but also are the neglected ones in our day. Jesus, as was true of the prophets, seemed to be partial, but His and their seeming partiality really stemmed from their impartiality. Jesus went about doing good. He was no respecter of persons. He could not be otherwise and reveal His Father and our Heavenly Father. The classic statement of Peter in the house of Cornelius was: "Truly I perceive that God shows no partiality" (Acts 10:34). This is a recurring emphasis in both Testaments.

Will you not agree that there has been entirely too much of a tendency in the contemporary world and even in contemporary churches to reverse the order of the concern of Jesus and the prophets? Too many churches seem to seek primarily the people who "can contribute something to the church" rather than majoring on reaching people who need the ministry of the church. When a worker with boys mentioned to a church secretary his interest in two boys and their families, she said, "They are

not our kind of people." Can you imagine Jesus ever saying that about any individual or family?

As Christians, we have and should declare a message of
reconciliation of man to God and man to man;[2] we also
have and should perform a personal ministry of reconciliation. If we are serious about a ministry of reconciliation, we should seek as best we can to go about doing
good. This will result, among other blessings, in our
churches moving toward the New Testament *koinonía,*
which knows nothing of cultural and racial barriers. This
will mean that we will need to beware of the contemporary emphasis on the homogeneous concept of the
church. Such an emphasis may help to enlist some people.
However, ideally, a Christian church should be without
class distinctions, composed of men and women, boys and
girls of various colors, cultures, and classes. The experience that makes them or should make them one is the fact
that they have all been made new creatures through their
union with the resurrected Christ.

Another way of underscoring the same emphasis is to
say that, through our experience of union with Christ, we
have entered into the family of God. As one family, we
should treat each other as brothers and sisters. Even those
who have not come into the spiritual family of God should
be treated as potential brothers and sisters. Do we do
that? Have some of us let our affluence or our poverty
blind us to the needs of other classes, cultures, and colors?

What about your church and mine? How close have
they come to the divine ideal for the church? Are there
some in the community who are not really welcome or
free to come to our church? Let me share with you one
experience. Mrs. D. and her husband were members of
the church. She had undergone some mental problems
and had spent short periods of time in a state mental

hospital. She and her husband were not attending the worship services of the church. When approached about it, her statement was that, when she was having her problems she had more sympathy and understanding from her non-Christian friends than from her fellow church members.

She and her husband returned for a few worship services but dropped out again. When visited, her statement was, "We do not feel that the folks up there want us." She agreed that this was not true of everyone in the church, but the visitor could not say that it was not true of some. Some might say that the responsibility was largely Mrs. D.'s and her husband's. However, Christians in general should be sensitive regarding the feelings of those who have been ill or who may be unusually sensitive for some other reason.

Senator Mark Hatfield has asked some questions that individual Christians and churches need to ask and seek to answer honestly: "What has happened? *Has* the church failed in its mission? *Has* the church lost its impetus to help troubled and hungry people? . . . Do we assume the responsibility to meet the needs of the whole community in which we live and even of the world, of which we are a part?"[3] Also, as Hatfield suggests, when it says in the Bible "God so loved the world" it means all the people of the world.

Billy Graham has expressed it:

> The blood of Christ makes us all equal.
> One tongue, one language, one race. . . .
> It doesn't matter what your skin color is.
> It doesn't matter what your social background is,
>   or your national background.
> We are in the body of Christ, we're all one.

By Identifying with Those Who Hurt

Nothing in the Scriptures reveals more clearly the fact that Jesus dignified or lifted the level of humanity than the fact that He identified with people who hurt. This fact is underscored by the kind of life He lived as He walked among people.

When someone reported to Jesus that His mother and brothers were seeking to get to Him but could not because of the crowd around Him, He asked, "Who is my mother, and who are my brothers?" The Bible says, "And stretching out his hand toward his disciples, he said, 'Here are my mother and my brothers! For whoever does the will of my Father in heaven is my brother, and sister, and mother'" (Matt. 12:48-50; see Mark 3:33-34; Luke 8:19-21). In other words, Jesus had a spiritual family as well as a natural family. Is this not true of many of us as Christians? There are occasions when we feel closer to some brothers and sisters in Christ than we do to our brothers and sisters by natural birth.

On another occasion, Jesus identified with a child, and children were generally among the underprivileged of Jesus' day. The disciples had inquired about who was greatest in the Kingdom. He placed a child in their midst and among other things said, "Whoever humbles himself like this child, he is the greatest in the kingdom of heaven" (Matt. 18:1-4). This, according to Matthew's record, was the background for the statement by Jesus, "Whoever receives one such child in my name receives me" (v. 5). In the book *The Bible and Family Relations*, which I coauthored with William Tillman, are chapters on "Women" and "Children."[4] Each of these chapters includes rather concise statements about the relation to and teachings of Jesus concerning women and children.

Therefore, I decided not to have a chapter in this book on the relation to and teachings of Jesus concerning women and children.

There is no place in the New Testament where the identification of Jesus with those who hurt and the under-privileged is brought out more clearly than in what He said concerning the separation of the sheep and the goats as recorded in Matthew 25. We should be deeply grateful for each of the Synoptic Gospels. Although they record much of the same material, that material is presented with some distinctive emphases or insights. Each Gospel has some unique material that considerably enriches our knowledge concerning Jesus and His teachings. The reference to the separation of the sheep and goats is distinctly Matthew material (Matt. 25:31-46).

On the surface, the Matthew passage sounds like a reference to the final judgment ("Before him will be gathered all the nations"). From our perspective, however, it makes little if any difference whether the reference is to the general judgment at the end of time or not. We are concerned primarily with the basis for the judgment and the fact that the "Son of man" or "the King" identified Himself with those who hurt. The separation of the sheep and the goats at night was very familiar to the people to whom Jesus spoke. The animals might graze together during the day, as they still do in parts of the world, but they were separated at night.

According to Matthew, this statement by Jesus about the separation of the sheep and the goats was at the close of a series of parables. The separation may have been a parable; but it was more than a parable, as was true of many if not most of the parables of Jesus. Jesus used parables as teaching instruments to clarify and make more impressive many pivotal teachings. This parable, if it be a parable, underscores two or three great truths. One primary thrust is the basis for the separation. Closely related to that main thrust is that Jesus identified with the underprivileged and in a specific way with those who hurt.

What was the basis for the separation? This question may have a challenging and even a disturbing relevance for us. The separation was not on the basis of what the people believed, as important as that was. Also, it was not on the basis of their faithfulness to the formalities of their faith, though that is also important.

Remembering a statement Jesus made in the Sermon on the Mount may be helpful to us. He said that we could know false prophets—and He could have added the true prophets—by their fruit. He also said, "Not every one who says to me, "'Lord, Lord,'" shall enter the kingdom of heaven, but he who does the will of my father who is in heaven" (Matt. 7:21). We know from the teachings of Jesus and the life He lived that the will of the Father is that we go about doing good. Matthew 25:31-46 clearly indicates some of the things we should do in order to be "going about doing good." They also indicate the kind of lives we must live if we expect Jesus' "well done" at the end of the journey. There is a tremendous challenge in these verses if we will meditate on them and let them search our souls.

Another truth revealed in these verses, and possibly the main thrust for the purpose of our study, is the fact that Jesus, as the Son of man or the King, identified with those who hurt: the hungry, the thirsty, the stranger, the naked, the sick, and those in prison. He said, "I was hungry and you gave me food," and so forth (vv. 35-36). The righteous or the ones who had heard His words of commendation asked, "When did we see thee hungry and feed thee?"

The goats or those condemned asked a similar question. The reply was, "Truly, I say to you, as you did it [did it not] to one of the least of these my brethren, you did to me" (Matt. 25:40,45). David Moberg's book with the simple title *Inasmuch* is based on the verse, "Inasmuch as ye have done it unto one of the least of these my brethren, ye have done it unto me" (Matt. 25:40; see 45, KJV). Notice the reference to "one of the least of these" and that they are referred to as "my brethren." Relationships and values in the family of God are not based on worldly status.

There is one other truth—at least implied in Matthew 25—that is not directly related to the purpose of this chapter. It is the fact that both those who heard "Come, . . . inherit the kingdom prepared for you" and "Depart from me, you cursed" (vv. 34,41) asked when they had served or not served the Lord. They were unconscious of the great truth that we serve or fail to serve Him as we serve those He would serve if He were personally here. The greatest servants of God are unconscious of their saintliness. That which naturally flows from our lives counts most with our Heavenly Father. The more mature we are in the Christian faith, the more clearly we will realize that the expression of the Christian life flows from within as a product of our union with and response to the indwelling Christ.

By His Death

This chapter on the fact that Jesus dignified humanity would not be complete without a brief statement about the relation of His death to the value that He and the Father gave to humanity. For Him and the Father, men and women, boys and girls were worth dying for. And possibly we should remember that He gave His life for sinners "dead in trespasses and sins." This fact, among other things, gives an innate dignity to all people regardless of their relationship to and attitude toward Him and the Father.

Jesus recognized, and we His followers should, that human beings are created in the image of God. This fact gives to humanity, in contrast to the rest of God's creation, dignity and worth. Although that image has been marred by sin, it has not and cannot be totally destroyed by sin. There is enough of the image left to serve as a point of contact for the message of redemption.

The preceding implies that one purpose of Jesus' death on the cross was the restoration of the defaced or marred image of God. In other words, through the death of Christ, a way was opened for men and women, boys and girls, to return to God and have that image restored. There is a sense in which the full restoration of the image is a process. As we mature in our relation to the indwelling Christ and in our obedience to Him, we, through God's grace, will more and more fully reveal the true image of God. The full achievement will not be complete until we awake in His likeness at the end of the journey. Then we will, in the fullest sense, be in the family of God, revealing the likeness of the One with whom we have been brought into full fellowship.

Possibly a word of caution should be inserted. Unfortunately, church membership should not be and cannot be equated with being in the true family of God. We should guard against any self-righteous spirit. We should be concerned about the entirely too-loose way that many of our churches accept new members, including those who come by profession of faith. Some of us fear that some are coming into our churches—and they are not all children —who have never had real life-changing experiences of the resurrected Christ coming into their lives. Paul spoke of "Christ in you, the hope of glory" (Col. 1:27). If there are such in your church and mine, they may hear at the end of the journey, "Depart from me." What a tragedy! Who is responsible? Could it be that we and our churches must bear part of the responsibility?

By this we may be sure that we are in him: he who says he abides in him ought to walk in the same way in which he walked (1 John 2:5-6, author's italics).

By this we know that we are in Him: the one who says he abides in Him ought himself to walk in the same manner as He walked (1 John 2:5-6, NASB, author's italics).

How much do we walk as He walked or lived in relation to people in general? What is our attitude toward and relation to the poor, the hungry, the handicapped, the underprivileged in general? Can it be said truthfully that we go about doing good, that we are increasingly walking as Jesus walked?

How do you react to the following quotation from George F. MacLeod?

I simply argue that the Cross be raised again at the centre of the market-place as well as on the steeple of the church. I am recovering the claim that Jesus was not crucified in a cathedral between two candles, but on a cross between two thieves; on the town garbage-heap; at a crossroad so cosmopolitan that they had to write his title in Hebrew and in Latin and in Greek . . . at the kind of place where cynics talk smut, and thieves curse, and soldiers gamble. Because that is where He died. And that is what He died about. And that is where churchmen should be and what churchmenship should be about.[5]

Notes

1. Walter Rauschenbusch, *The Social Principles of Jesus* (New York: Methodist Book Concern, 1916), p. 19.

2. Here and in most other places *man* does not refer to male in contrast to female but to man in contrast to God. In the record of creation, the Bible says, "So God created man in his own image, in the image of God he created him; male and female he created them" (Gen. 1:27).

3. Mark Hatfield, *Conflict and Conscience* (Waco: Word Books, 1971), p. 57.

4. T. B. Maston and William Tillman, *The Bible and Family Relations* (Nashville: Broadman Press, 1983).

5. George F. MacLeod, *Only One Way Left* (Glasgow: The Iona Community, 1956), p. 38.

4

He Included Samaria

Another evidence of the fact that Jesus went about doing good was Jesus' attitude toward the prejudice of the Jews against the Samaritans. The general consensus was that the Jews had no dealings with the Samaritans. In contrast, Jesus was interested in and concerned about all kinds of people, including the Samaritans.

Jews Versus Samaritans

During the divided kingdom, the capital of the Northern Kingdom was Samaria, and the capital of the Southern Kingdom was Jerusalem. The name *Samaria* was frequently applied to the Northern Kingdom and not exclusively to its capital. Also, the name *Samaritans* was used to refer to the inhabitants of the Northern Kingdom (see 2 Kings 17:24-28; 23:18-19).

When the Northern Kingdom fell, many of the inhabitants were carried into captivity. Some of the poorer people were left behind to till the soil and tend the vineyards. The king of Assyria brought people in from a number of other areas and placed them in the cities of Samaria (2 Kings 17:24). Those who were sent in brought with them competing customs and traditions. They intermingled and evidently intermarried with the Samaritans who were left behind. Some have suggested that the people of

Samaria became a "heterogeneous conglomerate" who neglected the Temple and after the fall of the Southern Kingdom ignored the desolation of Jerusalem.

It does seem, however, that the religion of the Samaritans continued to be, at least to some degree, Jewish. When they offered to share in the rebuilding of the Temple, they said, "Let us build with you; for we worship your God as you do, and we have been sacrificing to him" (Ezra 4:2). Their offer of help was declined. After that the Samaritans discouraged the Jews who were rebuilding the Temple. Whether the enmity that developed between the Jews and the Samaritans stemmed from this refusal of the proferred help, that enmity had become proverbial in the days of Jesus. The Jews had no dealings with the Samaritans. Some Jewish men thanked the Lord that they had not been born a woman, a slave, or a Samaritan.

Doubtlessly, one source of enmity was the keen rivalry that developed between the Northern Kingdom and the Southern Kingdom previous to the fall of the Northern Kingdom. Also, after the refusal of the proferred help, a place of worship was built on Mount Gerizim which became a competitor to the Temple at Jerusalem. This is the background for the statement by the Samaritan woman at the well: "Our Fathers worshiped on this mountain; and you say that in Jerusalem is the place where men ought to worship" (John 4:20). Jacob's well still stands at the foot of Mount Gerizim. It is possible that, as the woman said this, she pointed to the mount or waved her hand in that direction. By erecting a rival place of worship, the Samaritans had become a competing religious group. There is no area where emotions are aroused more easily or deeply than where religious practices and values are involved.

The Attitude of Jesus

Jesus revealed that His attitude toward the Samaritans was not typical of most Jews. Jesus had no national and racial prejudices. He revealed this attitude at different times under varying circumstances which is relevant for human relations in general and race relations in particular. As is true of social and cultural prejudice in general, the unfriendly attitude of Jews and Samaritans was not a one-way street.

There is some evidence in the New Testament of an unfriendly attitude of Samaritans toward the Jews. At least one clearly recognized case of this in the life and ministry of Jesus was when the people of a Samaritan village refused to receive Jesus and His disciples. He had "sent messengers ahead . . . to make ready for him" (Luke 9:51-53) and his disciples. The people of that Samaritan village "would not receive him, because his face was set toward Jerusalem" (v. 53). In other words, he was going by Mount Gerizim, the place of worship for the Samaritans, and going to Jerusalem to worship.

Usually Jews going from Galilee to Jerusalem for worship purposes did not go via Samaria. They took a longer route, crossing the Jordan in Galilee and going down the east side of the river. Notice the marked contrast in the reaction to the refusal by Jesus and by John and James. These two disciples may have reflected the general reaction of the other disciples. The reaction of John and James, expressed in a question to Jesus, was, "Do you want us to bid fire come down from heaven and consume them?" (Luke 9:54). Possibly their recent experience on the mount of transfiguration when Moses and Elijah had appeared and talked to Jesus concerning "his departure, which he was to accomplish at Jerusalem" (Luke 9:31) was the occasion for their reference to Elijah's experience (2 Kings 1:10-12). They, as was doubtlessly true of the other disciples, were as ready to take offense as the Samaritan villagers were to give it.

Jesus had an entirely different attitude. After He had rebuked John and James, "They went on to another village" (v. 56). How much do we have of the "went on to another village" spirit? It is interesting to note that one of these "sons of thunder" (Mark 3:17), after he had appropriated more of the spirit of Jesus, went with his friend Peter on a mission to Samaria (Acts 8:14-25). At the close of that missionary journey, the Record says, "They returned to Jerusalem, preaching the gospel to many villages of the Samaritans" (v. 25). Is it possible that one of those villages was where John and James had asked about calling down fire to consume it?

There are some other recorded incidents when Jesus revealed His attitude toward the Samaritans. On one occasion, Jesus had a lengthy conversation with some of the Jews. Rather typically, when they could not answer Him, they attempted to label Him. They asked, "Are we not right in saying that you are a Samaritan and have a demon?" (John 8:48). They could think of no meaner thing to say. He answered the last portion of the accusation but ignored the charge that He was a Samaritan. Why did He ignore that part of the accusation? Is it possible that He made no attempt to answer it because to Him it was not distasteful to be called a Samaritan? This incident may have provided, at least to some degree, the background for Peter's statement, "When he was reviled, he did not revile in return" (1 Pet. 2:23).

Another time Jesus "was passing along between Samaria and Galilee. And as he entered a village, he was met by ten lepers, who stood at a distance." They cried, "Jesus,

Master, have mercy on us." He told them to go to the priests; while, in obedience to his instructions, they were on their way, they were all healed. Only one returned and thanked Jesus for his healing, and the Record says, "Now he was a Samaritan" (Luke 17:11-16). Then Jesus remarked, "Were not ten cleansed? Where are the nine? Was no one found to return and give praise to God except this foreigner?" (vv. 17-18).

The concluding word of Jesus to the Samaritan was, "Rise and go your way; your faith has made you well" (v. 19). The fact that Jesus healed the Samaritan as well as the other nine and the additional fact that He called attention to the Samaritan underscores the attitude of Jesus toward Samaritans. He was no respecter of persons. He reached out to all kinds of people. In being impartial, Jesus seemed to be partial to the underprivileged of His day. No group in that day was more underprivileged, from the Jewish perspective, than the Samaritans. This Samaritan was also a leper. Lepers as a group were the most avoided people of that day. They needed desperately someone to understand that they, like all men and women, boys and girls, were created in the image of God. As such, they had and still have innate dignity and worth.

We may not have many physical lepers in our society, but we do have people who are treated as lepers. They are avoided by most people, particularly by the middle and upper classes. Also, they are avoided too frequently by those of us who are followers of Jesus, who reached out in love to all kinds of people. Few things will reveal more about our relationship with Jesus, our being possessed by the Spirit, than our attitude toward and treatment of the moral lepers, the social outcasts of our society.

In the light of the spirit and attitude of Jesus, one incident that creates some problems. When Jesus sent out the twelve, He instructed them not to go to the Gentiles in general and to the Samaritans in particular (Matt. 10:5). How can we explain that restriction, particularly in the light of Jesus' own attitude toward and ministry to the Samaritans?

There are two possible explanations. One is the fact that the good news of the promised Messiah was to be preached first to the Jews. They were to have the first chance to accept Him. The other explanation for the prohibition, and possibly the correct or main one, was the fact that the twelve were not adequately prepared at that time. As A. B. Bruce said: It is possible Jesus knew that their hearts were too narrow, their prejudices too strong; there was too much of the Jew, too little of the Christian, in their characters.

A basic and valid principle of interpretation is that any one Scripture should be interpreted in the light of the totality of the teachings of the Scriptures. This one principle would force us to conclude that whatever limitation was placed on the twelve was temporary. We also know that soon after Jesus' crucifixion and resurrection some of these same disciples made a "missionary journey" into some of the villages of Samaria.

The Concern of Jesus

Jesus was concerned for all kinds of people and particularly for the neglected, for those who felt the prejudice of some particular group or of most people. The Samaritans in the days of Jesus were certainly in that group. No one incident in the life and ministry of Jesus reveals more of His concern than His conversation with the Samaritan woman at the well. On that occasion, He ignored or violated more than one prejudice of most Jews. She was a woman. She was a Samaritan woman. She was a sinful

Samaritan woman. But Jesus never permitted race, sex, or moral condition to prevent Him from reaching out in understanding compassion to one who hurt and particularly one who was responsive to His presence.

Now, let us reexamine some of the particulars of this striking occasion. The immediate background of this experience says that "He [Jesus] had to pass through Samaria" (John 4:4). Why did He have to? It is true that it was the nearest route from Galilee to Jerusalem, but it was not the route that the Jews ordinarily used. Did Jesus have "to pass through Samaria" because He was in a hurry to get to Jerusalem? On the surface, this would not seem to be the real reason for Jesus and His disciples going through Samaria. After all, He remained in Samaria for two days after His experience with the Samaritan woman at Jacob's well.

Was there a spiritual urgency that compelled Him to go through Samaria? There is no way to know for sure, but what happened at Jacob's well and its consequences could suggest that the needs of the woman and her neighbors created the desire or compulsion to go through Samaria. Whatever the reason for going through Samaria, we do know that Jesus was weary and "sat down beside the well" (v. 6) and that it "was about the sixth hour [or "about noon," NEB]." The disciples had gone into the city to buy food.

While Jesus sat there, a Samaritan woman came to draw water. Jesus took the initiative and for a Jew did a very unusual thing—He asked her to give Him a drink. Jesus saw the woman at the well as a person created in the image of God. It may be true, as has been suggested, that it was a greater wonder to the disciples that Jesus talked with a woman than that He talked with a Samaritan. But Jesus never permitted sex, race, or moral condition to

keep Him from meeting the needs and particularly the
spiritual needs of men and women.

Jesus introduced the Samaritan woman to the living
water which permanently satisfies the thirst of the human
heart. The thirst that is permanently satisfied by this living water is the hunger or thirst for "eternal life" (v. 14).
This experience, in reality, creates within the newborn
child of God a hunger and thirst that will never be completely satisfied until he or she awakes at the end of life
in the likeness of Christ.

Jesus asked the woman to bring her husband to Him.
Her reply was that she had no husband. When Jesus told
her that she had had five husbands and that the one she
now had was not her husband, she said, "Sir, I perceive
that you are a prophet" (v. 19). Then she introduced the
question of the proper place to worship God—Mount
Gerizim or Jerusalem. Jesus said to her, and would say to
us, that the claims of rival sacred places—Gerizim and
Jerusalem—were and are swept away in the revelation
that God is spirit and can be worshiped anywhere. The
place does not make worship acceptable; motive and
spirit make worship acceptable or unacceptable. He said,
"God is spirit, and those who worship him must worship
in spirit and truth" (v. 24).

The woman said she knew the Messiah was coming.
Then Jesus made the startling statement: "I who speak to
you am he" (v. 26). This is the first time, so far as we know,
that Jesus specifically revealed that He was the promised
Messiah.

Many of the Samaritan were responsive to the woman's
report that she had met and talked with the promised
Messiah. At their request, Jesus remained in their village
for two days, and many of the people believed the message He proclaimed to them. What a short time—only two

days—but what a long time for Jesus, who had a sense of urgency, to tarry in one village.

Think what would be missing from the Gospel story if Jesus had not stopped that day at Jacob's well. How grateful we ought to be for His ministry among the Samaritans. This was another outstanding example of His wayside ministry. He went about doing good. No wonder the first notable revival outside of Jerusalem was among the people of Samaria (Acts 8:4-25). They had been prepared for the gospel of Christ by His visit with the Samaritan woman at Jacob's well, by His staying in their midst for two days, and by His contact with and attitudes toward the Samaritan people in general.

The Teachings of Jesus

Jesus not only included Samaria and Samaritans in His concern for people but also made a Samaritan the hero of one of His greatest stories or parables (Luke 10:25-37). Jesus never did anything by accident. He deliberately selected the Samaritan as the hero of the parable. When Jesus said, "But a Samaritan" (Luke 10:33), the lawyer's shock probably showed in his face and the audience was probably disgusted. We call the hero the "good Samaritan"; but to most of those who originally heard the story from the lips of Jesus, there were no good Samaritans.

The man who had been robbed was the only one in the parable or story who was not identified by race or vocation. Was he a Jew or a Samaritan? Was he a good man or an evil man? The only description was that he was a man who was in need. Everything else was and should be secondary for us.

The priest and the Levite may have an important message for many of us who are church members and claim to be followers of Jesus. They did not hurt the man in need; neither did they help him. They refused to get mixed up in the unpleasant task of helping a man in need. They stood aloof from both robbery and service.

A group of students in the Arab Baptist Seminary at Beirut, Lebanon, were asked: "If Jesus were giving or repeating that parable to a group in the United States, who would be the hero?" Very promptly, two or three of the students answered, "A Black man." Then they were asked, "If Jesus were speaking to one of your churches, who would be the "good Samaritan"? One student promptly answered, "A Jew," while another said, "Or a Moslem."

We should remember that the parable of the good Samaritan was given in response to the lawyer's question, "Teacher, what shall I do to inherit eternal life?" (v. 25). Then, as a good teacher frequently does, Jesus asked him to answer his own question. The lawyer gave the rather common summary of the law: "You shall love the Lord with all your heart, and with all your soul, and with all your strength, and with all your mind, and your neighbor as yourself" (v. 27; see Deut. 6:5; Lev. 19:18). Jesus' replied, "You have answered right; do this, and you will live" (v. 28). Then the lawyer asked, "And who is my neighbor?" (v. 29). The lawyer wanted Jesus to build a fence that would limit neighbor and hence limit love, but Jesus never placed any limits on His basic teachings. The lawyer's question was background for the parable. Jesus did not directly answer the lawyer's question. If there is an implied answer, even indirectly, in the parable it would be, Your neighbor is anyone in need.

The significance of the parable is considerably increased by the fact that the question was asked by a Jewish lawyer and by the usual assumption that the victim was a Jew. The existence of the feud between the Jews and the Samaritans enormously increases the point of the parable. This is one of the two places in all of the New Testament where compassion is attributed to a human. The other is the father of the prodigal son (Luke 15:20). These, two of the greatest parables of Jesus, could properly be called parables of compassion.

The priest and the Levite saw the man, but passed by on the other side. In contrast, the Samaritan did what a Jew would not have expected him to do. He acted or reacted that day as men and women should when they discover a fellow human being in distress. The key to what the Samaritan did was the fact that he had compassion.

Jesus pressed home the lesson of the story. The lawyer had asked, "Who is my neighbor?" Jesus asked the lawyer a much more important question: "Which of these three, do you think, proved neighbor to the man who fell among the robbers?" (v. 36). The lawyer evidently could not rid himself of all his prejudice. He could not bring himself to say, "The Samaritan." His reply was: "The one who showed mercy on him" (v. 37). One possible purpose Jesus had in mind in telling this beautiful parable was that the lawyer and other Jews might see the foolishness and sinfulness of their prejudice against the Samaritans.

A former student and teaching colleague suggests some contemporary applications of the parable of the good Samaritan: (1) We should not let religious duties or activities prevent us from being helpful to those in need. (2) We should not let religious or social differences prevent us from being helpful to those in need. (3) Being a good neighbor involves inconvenience.

The same former student observed that the parable of the good Samaritan is particularly significant because of the admonition of Jesus to the lawyer: "Go and do likewise" (v. 37). Its importance is underscored because it is the only recorded incident where Jesus referred to the behavior of a person as an example for others to follow.

What did the Samaritan do that is an appropriate pattern for others? To begin with, his service was personal. He went to the victim, treated his wounds, put him on his beast, took him to the inn, told the innkeeper to care for him, and promised to check about the man when he returned. Too many of us are prone to serve by proxy—pay someone else to do it for us. An unknown sage put it like this: "We may pay someone to do good works, but we cannot pay someone to do *our* work."

Furthermore, the good Samaritan's ministry was unselfish. Too frequently even the good that many of us do is not properly motivated. Also, the Samaritan's service or ministry was thorough. What else could he have done? Haskell Miller has suggested that the parable of the good Samaritan has possibly done more to encourage human compassion and helpfulness "than any other single influence in all of religion, literature, or history."

The Commission of Jesus

Matthew 28:19-20 is generally identified as the Great Commission. There are other places, however, in the Gospels where Jesus stated something comparable to the Great Commission (see Mark 16:15-18; Luke 24:46-49, and John 20:21-22). The disciples were to go into the world with the good news.

The Book of Acts includes what might be a restatement of the Commission: "You shall receive power when the Holy Spirit has come upon you; and you shall be my witnesses in Jerusalem and in Judea and Samaria and to the end of the earth" (Acts 1:8). These were the parting words of the resurrected Christ to the disciples. Also, this instruction gives a preview of the content of the Book of

Acts. Luke, in writing Acts, seems to have followed this outline: Jerusalem, Judea, and Samaria, and the uttermost part of the earth.

But why was Samaria included in a special way? Certainly "the end of the earth" or "all nations" (Matt. 28:19) included Samaria. One possible reason for including Samaria was its proximity to Jerusalem and Judea. But the resurrected Christ may have said "and Samaria" because of the prejudice of the Jews against the Samaritans. If they would go to Samaria with the "good news" of salvation, they would go anywhere. Even if the primary reference was to the proximity of Samaria, the strongest prejudice of the Jews was against Samaritans.

Where is our Samaria? If the reference is to those living close by, are we witnessing to those by word of mouth and by the life we live? If the reference is primarily to those against whom we are strongly prejudiced—whether color, class, or condition of life—are we sharing the good news with them? What is the predominant attitude in our churches? Do their spirits draw or repel people?

We should not forget that Jesus said, "And you shall be *my* witnesses" (author's italics). This can be interpreted in two ways: (1) They were to witness to others about and for Him; (2) as witnesses they were His; they belonged to Him; He had purchased them, as He has us, with His death on the cross. Really, it makes little difference how the statement is interpreted. Both are true in the deepest sense. They belonged and we belong to Him. Belonging to Him, they and we should witness to and for Him wherever they were and we are.

There was no place in the life, ministry, and teaching of Jesus for a "we-they" division. Many interracial problems have their roots in the "we are-they are" psychology. Those of the "we" group usually belong to the majority and consider themselves superior. Those of the "they" group are excluded from many of the privileges of the "we" group. "They" are usually considered to be inferior.

Regardless of how serious the present racial and cultural situation may be or may become, this much is certainly true: the we-they division does not, or at least should not, belong within the Christian fellowship. The only division among people in a thoroughly Christian group or society would be divisions based upon moral conduct and spiritual condition and even these would be treated as potential brothers in Christ, as actual or potential members of the family of God.

Do we have a Samaria, a "they" group, in our vocabulary? If so, what is the basis for it—color, economic condition, cultural differences, and so forth? How willing are we to cross any barrier to minister to those in need? If we go about doing good as Jesus did, we will not permit any human difference to prevent us from reaching out and ministering to those who are in need.

By this we may be sure that we are in him: he who says he abides in him ought to walk in the same way in which he walked (1 John 2:5-6, author's italics)

Here is the test by which we can make sure that we are in him: whoever claims to be dwelling in him, binds himself to live as Christ himself lived (1 John 2:5-6, NEB, author's italics)

5
He Emphasized a Distinctive Life-style

When we understand the different aspects of the life-style that Jesus emphasized and demonstrated, we may conclude that it was not only challenging to His original disciples but also is or should be equally challenging to us, His contemporary followers. The world in which most of us live is drastically different from the world in which Jesus and His original disciples lived. This does not mean, however, that the kind of life-style advocated and demonstrated by Jesus is not applicable to us.

We can discover the kind of life-style Jesus emphasized by what He taught and by the kind of life He lived. Jesus never suggested and never will suggest a way of life which is inconsistent with His life and teachings. He continues to say, "Follow me."

Its Content

Some of the plainest and most challenging statements made by Jesus were related, directly or indirectly, to a relatively simple life-style. The word *relatively* is necessary in the preceding sentence. The life-style of any person or society is always more or less relative. For example, a simple life-style at one time and/or in one culture might not be considered simple at another time or in a different culture. It does seem clear, however, that Jesus would advocate a simple life-style relative to when and where a follower of His lives. In other words, what might be considered a simple life-style in the United States and most Western European nations would not be considered simple in most other areas of the world.

Furthermore, even in the United States, a life-style that might be considered quite simple in our day might have seemed rather elaborate in the pioneer days of our nation. Even in the contemporary period in our nation, there are geographic areas where a "simple life-style" would be quite different from other areas or sections of the same city.

Regardless of how we define "simple life-style," Jesus emphasized it for His followers. It is a message that many of us need. He stressed that life-style in various ways— some direct and others more indirect. This emphasis is quite evident in His parables. Some of His most challenging teachings are revealed in and through His parables. Most of them were drawn from the everyday experiences of the common people. For example, the parables recorded in Matthew 13 were largely familiar to those to whom Jesus spoke on that occasion.

The preceding was certainly true of "A sower went out to sow" (Matt. 13:3; Mark 4:3; Luke 8:5). Jesus may have actually pointed to a sower as He told the parable. Whether He did or not, the people who heard Him that day understood what He was saying. Sowing seed had been the actual experience or at least the observation of most who heard Him on that occasion.

Matthew 13 records several other parables. Most of them were from the everyday experiences and/or observations of the common people. This was certainly true of the parable of the weeds (Matt. 13:24-30,36-43), the mustard seed (Matt. 13:31-32; Mark 4:30-32), the leaven (Matt.

13:33). The hidden treasure, the pearl of great price, and the net full of fish (Matt. 13:44-50) might not have been as well-known experiences.

Jesus not only used parables drawn from the simple things of life but also, more directly, used simple everyday things of life to underscore His emphasis on a simple life-style. In the Sermon on the Mount, immediately after the Beatitudes, He said to the disciples, "You are the salt of the earth; . . . You are the light of the world" (Matt. 5:13-14). He followed with a few pointed comments.

He used many other simple, everyday things thoroughly familiar to the people to whom He spoke, most of whom were from among the poor or common people. He spoke of the birds in the air (Matt. 6:26), the lilies of the field (Matt. 6:28-29), the lost coin (Luke 15:8-9), and the lost sheep (Luke 15:6; see Matt. 10:6; 15:24), the separation of the sheep and the goats at night (Matt. 25:32-33). He called attention to the widow who cast all that she had into the treasury (Mark 12:42-43; Luke 21:2-3). These and many other illustrations were used by Jesus as He emphasized the simple things of life.

Jesus not only emphasized a relatively simple life-style but also emphasized a number of additional concepts which would mean a distinctive life-style for His followers. For example, there is enough in the brief Sermon on the Mount (Matt. 5—7) to challenge any serious followers of Jesus for the rest of their earthly journey. No passage in the entire Bible contains as many elements of a distinctive Christian life-style as the Sermon on the Mount.

The sermon or message opens with the Blesseds or Beatitudes. Most of these differ considerably from the way most contemporary followers of Jesus would state them. They suggest a distinctive life-style. This is particularly true if we use Luke's evident record of the same teachings. He did not spiritualize the Beatitudes. For example, he reported Jesus as saying, "Blessed are you poor, for yours is the kingdom of God" (Luke 6:20) rather than "Blessed are the poor in spirit, for theirs is the kingdom of heaven" (Matt. 5:3). Instead of saying, "Blessed are those who hunger and thirst for righteousness, for they shall be satisfied" (Matt. 5:6), Luke simply says, "Blessed are you that hunger now, for you shall be satisfied" (6:21). Of course, it should be recognized that Luke may nowhere have been referring to the Sermon on the Mount. Jesus, as is true of any superb teacher, repeated from time to time the same teaching or emphasis. Every Beatitude, whether we use Matthew or Luke, will reveal a distinctive life-style—distinctive for our day as well as for the original disciples.

The Beatitudes are followed in Matthew with a declaration that the disciples were "salt" and "light." The conclusion of Jesus to the latter is a continuing challenge to any who claim to be His disciples or followers. He made the obvious observation that men did not light a lamp and place it under a basket. Rather, it was supposed to be put "on a stand, and it gives light to all in the house" (v. 15). Jesus continued by saying something which will deeply touch every sensitive Christian: "Let your light so shine before men, that they may see your good works and give glory to your Father who is in heaven" (Matt. 5:16).

The remainder of the Sermon on the Mount contains a number of emphases that, if followed consistently, would contribute to a distinctive life-style. For example, Jesus explained to the disciples what it meant to be obedient to the Law. Among other things, He made obedience to the Law primarily inner rather than outer. For example, one could commit adultery by looking lustfully at a woman (Matt. 5:28).

Space will not permit reference in detail to the additional emphases in the sermon that, taken seriously and followed consistently, would require a distinctive life-style. Some of those additional emphases are: divorce (5: 31-32); oaths (5:33-37); nonresistance (5:38-42); love of enemy (5:43-47); unpretentiousness in giving of alms, prayer, fasting (Matt. 6:1-18).

Also, in Matthew 6 (vv. 9-15) is recorded the Model Prayer, which is remarkably concise and yet a remarkably comprehensive prayer. It starts with the all-inclusive "Our Father," which presents a challenge to many children of God—young and old. It includes all who are in the spiritual family of God regardless of color, culture, condition of life, or denomination. Unless we can sincerely pray "Our Father," we have no sound basis to say or pray "My Father."

Note that, after "Hallowed by thy name," the first petition of the prayer is, "Thy kingdom come,/Thy will be done,/On earth as it is in heaven." This should be the first petition, whether or not verbalized, in the prayer of any child of God. Until we have prayed that prayer, we have no right to pray:

> Give us this day our daily bread;
> And forgive us our debts,
>   As we also have forgiven our debtors;
> And lead us not into temptation,
>   But deliver us from evil.

Notice particularly the petition regarding forgiveness. This is the only petition in the prayer about which there is some comment. What a challenge it implies! It plainly says that the Father's forgiveness of us as His children depends on our forgiveness of those who have sinned

against us. It is the forgiving who can be and are forgiven.
Also, the forgiven should be forgiving.

Matthew 6 contains the fullest recorded statement of
Jesus concerning treasures or material things. I doubt if
there are many elements in the teachings of Jesus needed
more by contemporary Christians, particularly in the in-
dustrial nations of the West. Why not look over the passage carefully and seek honestly to let its message or
messages speak a word to you and yours? For example, we
find the statements, "Do not lay up for yourselves treasures on earth, . . . For where your treasure is, there will
your heart be also" (6:19-21); "No one can serve two mas-
ters; . . . You cannot serve God and mammon [Money,
NEB, NIV]" (6:24).

Then He told the disciples not to be anxious about what
they would eat, drink, or wear. He suggested that they
should observe the birds of the air and the lilies of the
field. The Heavenly Father cares for them. The disciples
were of much more value. Jesus' wonderful conclusion
was, "But seek first his kingdom and his righteousness,
and all these things shall be yours as well" (6:33). Pointed
questions for you and me are, What place does the rule,
the reign, the kingdom of God have in our lives? Do we
seek it first? One additional question: Could it be that the
ineffectiveness of many of us as children of God is based
on or results from the limited place we give in our lives
to the will and purpose of the Heavenly Father?

The seventh chapter of Matthew can be summarized by
quoting a few statements, most of which introduce para-
graphs in the Revised Standard Version of the Bible.
Among these are the following: "Judge not, that you be
not judged" (v. 1); "Ask, and it will be given you" (v. 7);
"Beware of false prophets, . . . You will know them by
their fruits" (vv. 15-16); "Not every one who says to me,

'Lord, Lord,' shall enter the kingdom of heaven, but he who does the will of my Father who is in heaven" (v. 21); "Every one then who hears these words of mine and does them will be like a wise man who built his house upon the rock" (v. 24).

Is it any wonder that "when Jesus finished these sayings, the crowds were astonished at his teaching" (v. 28)? The more seriously you and I take Jesus' teachings in the sermon and seek to apply them in our daily lives, the more we will be astonished. Have you wondered at times what it might mean in your life as a professed follower of Christ if you lived fully the kind of life He would have you live? Most contemporary Christians would discover that consistently applying His teachings and spirit to our everyday lives would revolutionize and change the direction of our lives. If enough of us would seek seriously to be obedient to His teachings in the Sermon on the Mount, a real revolution would result in our churches which would deeply influence every phase of the Christian movement and the world in general.

Only a casual reading of the remainder of the Gospel of Matthew reveals a number of other teachings that, if followed, would result in a distinctive life-style, distinctive not only when compared to nonbelievers but also when compared to most church members. Why not read Matthew 8—28 and mark or check the teachings of Jesus which you think might result in a distinctive type of life? Or, even better, if you have a harmony of the Gospels, check through it for the distinctive contributions to a challenging life-style by each of the Gospel writers. In addition to previous suggestions, let us now consider a few additional teachings of major importance.

One of the bases for kinship with Jesus is: "Whoever does the will of my Father in heaven is my brother, and

sister, and mother" (Matt. 12:50; see Mark 3:35; Luke
8:21). Another striking teaching is the fact that the sense
of the divine presence is the secret to the nonfretful heart:
"Take heart, it is I; have no fear" (Matt. 14:27; Mark 6:50;
John 6:20). Personally, a meaningful discovery was the
fact that there is no crucifixion or death without resurrection or the discovery of real life. To the degree that we
crucify self, take up a cross, and follow him, we discover
life at its fullest and best (See Matt. 16:24-25; Mark 8:34-
35; Luke 9:23-24). Closely akin to the preceding, if not
actually a different way of expressing the same basic truth,
is the fact that true humility results in greatness or exalta-
tion (Matt. 18:4; see Luke 14:11; 18:14). In other words,
the truly great are humble.

Its Demonstration

Jesus did not live like John the Baptist. Jesus followed
a more normal life-style than John, His forerunner. He
associated rather freely with all kinds of people. But over-
all, when compared to the life-style of most people, even
those with whom He associated, His was quite simple. The
charge that He was a glutton and a drunkard was false
although the remainder of the charge was accurate: "A
friend of tax collectors and sinners!" (Luke 7:34).

Jesus was laid in a manger at birth and buried in a
borrowed tomb. Instead of an offering of a lamb for purifi-
cation rites, Joseph and Mary took a pair of turtledoves to
the Temple (Luke 2:24). Carpenters may not have been
the poorest folk in the society of that day, but they were
certainly not wealthy. Being a carpenter's son, from the
viewpoint of many of Jesus' contemporaries, limited Him
in some ways. On one occasion when He had spoken to
those in "his own country," they marveled at his wisdom
and his "mighty works" and asked: "Is not this the carpen-

ter's son? Is not his mother called Mary? And are not his brothers James and Joseph and Simon and Judas? And are not all his sisters with us? Where then did this man get all this?" (Matt. 13:54-56; see Mark 6:2-3).

After the death of Joseph, we assume that Jesus, in harmony with the customs of that time, became head of the house. He doubtlessly continued to follow the carpenter's trade to help support His mother and family. His experiences as a carpenter possibly were the source of some of His metaphors. For example, He mentioned the kind of foundation on which a house should be built (Matt. 7:24-27).

Ronald Sider concluded that "Jesus' poverty is a hard historical fact unanimously portrayed in all four Gospels." He further said, "In order to understand its significance, it must be viewed in the light of Jewish piety in Jesus' day, according to which poverty was usually regarded a curse and wealth was praised as evidence of God's favour."[1] Many people today, including entirely too many Christians, still judge and evaluate poverty and wealth in the same way.

Henry van Dyke, a favorite writer and poet of a generation or two ago, captured something of the life-style of Jesus in the following:

> Born within the lowly stable,
> Where cattle around me stood,
> Trained a carpenter in Nazareth,
> I have tasted and found it good.
>
> Where the many toil together,
> There am I among my own;
> Where the tired workman sleepeth,
> There am I with him alone.

If you examine the additional teachings of Jesus concerning life-style, you will see that He fully demonstrated in His own life every truth He recommended or suggested to others. Just a relatively few examples: His followers were to be "the light of the world"; He was "the true light that enlightens every man [that] was coming into the world" (John 1:9). He told His disciples not to treasure the treasures of earth and told them that they could not serve two-masters—God and mammon or money. They should not be anxious about the necessities of life. They should seek first the kingdom, reign, or rule of God and simply trust Him to provide for them. Certainly, He lived with one dominant purpose in His life and with its resulting calm and nonfretfulness.

Jesus would suggest to us as Paul did to the Philippians:

> Let each of you look not only to his own interests, but also to the interests of others. Have this mind among yourselves, which is yours in Christ Jesus, who, though he was in the form of God, did not count equality with God a thing to be grasped, but emptied himself, taking the form of a servant, being born in the likeness of men. And being found in human form he humbled himself and became obedient unto death, even death on a cross (Phil. 2:4-8).

Also note what Paul said in verses 9-11:

> Therefore God has highly exalted him and bestowed on him the name which is above every name, that at the name of Jesus every knee should bow, in heaven and on earth, and under the earth, and every tongue confess that Jesus Christ is Lord, to the glory of God the Father.

Jesus also attempted to help His disciples understand that resurrection followed real crucifixion. He never spoke of His own crucifixion without in the same breath speaking of His resurrection. When crucified, He was laid in a borrowed tomb, but that tomb could not hold Him.

"Up from the grave he arose,/With a mighty triumph o'er his foes."

Its Application

The early church caught something of the life-style of Jesus. At least theirs was a relatively simple life-style. It seems that most of the new converts at Jerusalem were poor. Some were relatively well-to-do. Many of the latter shared what they had that the poor might be adequately cared for.

Something closely akin to Christian communism developed. It was a Christian-motivated, voluntary sharing with one another. The record in Acts says, "Now the company of those who believed were of one heart and soul, and no one said that any of the things which he possessed was his own, but they had everything in common" (Acts 4:32). It is interesting and should be challenging to read the very next verse: "And with great power the apostles gave their testimony to the resurrection of the Lord Jesus, and great grace was upon them all" (v. 33). Read verses 34-37 for the rest of the story.

This sharing was true in other churches who sent offerings to help care for the needy saints in Jerusalem. Such offerings were a major element in Paul's ministry. He encouraged the Christians at Rome to "contribute to the needs of the saints" and to "practice hospitality" (Rom. 12:13). Near the close of the epistle, he reported that he was "going to Jerusalem with aid for the saints" (Rom. 15:25). Paul added that those who were sending the aid were in debt to the saints of Jerusalem. The latter had shared spiritual blessings with those of Macedonia; the Macedonians "ought also to be of service to them in material blessings" (Rom. 15:27). Paul referred to the offering for the saints in both of the Corinthian epistles (1 Cor.

16:1; 2 Cor. 8:1-7; 9:1-5). It seems that most of the early
Christian converts not only in Jerusalem but elsewhere, as
is true today at home and particularly on mission fields,
were predominantly poorer people. Paul, in the very first
chapter of 1 Corinthians, reminded them that not many
of them were wise, powerful, or of noble birth (vv. 26-31).

From references previously given and from 1 Timothy
(5:8,16), the order of responsibility for the needy was and
still is: first, the natural family; second, the spiritual family
or the church; and last of all, the human family or community or state.

As has been emphasized over and over again through
the Christian centuries, the Christian is a citizen of two
worlds. This creates for the serious Christian a constant
tension. Being in this world or the world of "Caesar"
involves relations to the family, the state, the workaday
world, and so forth. But being a Christian, every relation
and responsibility one has as a citizen of this world should
be informed and influenced by the fact that one is also a
citizen of the kingdom of God. While as a citizen of this
world the responsibilities to this world should be taken
seriously, nevertheless, this world for a Christian should
always be considered "a tabernacle." We are strangers or
pilgrims here "within a foreign land." But let us never
forget as individual Christians and Christian churches
that, while we may be foreigners here, we are "here" and
should live as best we can distinctively Christian lifes.

Jacques Ellul, a popular French Protestant writer,
summed up the Christian's predicament as follows: "The
Christian who is involved in the natural history of this
world is involved in it as representing another order."[2]
He further suggested, as have others, that living in these
two worlds means inevitably that the Christian lives with
constant tension. The more serious one is about being a

real and not a merely nominal Christian, the deeper is one's conviction that the two kingdoms can never be equated. "The opposition between the world and the Kingdom of God is a total one." This even means that no achievement of ours and other Christians and/or their churches can or should be equated with the kingdom or rule of God. The latter will be ultimately achieved only by God Himself. But we should remember that there is no progress without some tension.

We need in our day to recover something of the nature and character of the early Christian fellowship. The Christians of New Testament days became well known as a caring and sharing fellowship. "Their faith produced a discernible lifestyle, a way of life, . . . visible to all. This different style of living . . . grew out of their faith and gave testimony to that faith. . . . Their love for God, for one another, and for the oppressed was central to their reputation."3 Jim Wallis also said, "The loss of a distinctively Christian lifestyle, has severely damaged our proclamation of the gospel."4

In another book, Wallis said some things that should disturb many contemporary Christians. His charge is that "today many who name the name of Christ have removed themselves from human hurt and suffering to places of relative comfort, safety. Many have sought to protect themselves and their families from the poor and wretched masses for whom Christ showed such primary concern."5 He also spoke of "the church's compassionless inactivity in relation to people who hurt" which he said is "a major obstacle to being faithful to the biblical mandates."

At home and particularly on the mission fields, upward mobility for Christians seems more or less inevitable. For example, the more serious Christians are about their responsibilities as citizens of the world, the more conscientious they are about their work or vocations, the more likely they will move up the economic and prestige ladder. What is needed to accompany this more or less inevitable upward mobility is a downward mobility to reach the underprivileged masses. This is needed by an increasing number of individual Christians but also by churches. If this is not done, a church ultimately will become more like a club for the privileged than a lighthouse to point the lost to a fuller and more meaningful and productive lives. Such a church will also tend increasingly to become like a cemetery rather than a marketplace alive with people of all ages and all classes.

Many of our churches, as well as many of their members, have become affluent. Some have suggested that many churches and their members cannot truthfully say, "[We] have no silver and gold," but neither can they say, "In the name of Jesus Christ of Nazareth, walk" (Acts 3:6). Too frequently our prosperity has robbed us and our churches of the compassion for suffering people and the sense of dependence on God for the power to heal the hurts of people.

There is an exhortation in Paul's Letter to the Romans which is a fitting climax and conclusion to this chapter on a distinctive life-style: "Do not be conformed to this world but be transformed by the renewal of your mind, that you may prove what is the will of God, what is good and acceptable and perfect" (Rom. 12:2). *The New English Bible* translates this verse as follows: "Adapt yourselves no longer to the pattern of this present world, but let your minds be remade and your whole nature thus transformed." Conformity is generally an accomplished fact. Transformation or nonconformity must be a progressive achievement, never fully attained, a constant challenge to churches and individual Christians. Unfortunately for the

latter, and we do not like to admit or say it, but too frequently his or her church will not be much help in the
struggle. Indeed, some contemporary churches have
become so captured by the spirit of the world that they
will add to the pressure on individual members to con-
form to the world and its standards of success.

Some may· be surprised that little attention has been
given to the prevalence of poverty and hunger in our
world. This has not been done to belittle the seriousness
of the problem. We should be concerned and should cooperate with others in relieving the terrible conditions in
which many people of the world live. Gandhi is supposed
to have said, "If God were to come to India today, He'd
come as bread." At least, He would seek to relieve their
needs.

The conviction behind the approach in this chapter is
that every child of God should follow a relatively simple
life-style and should seek to live a distinctly Christian life,
even if there were no hungry people in our world. The
prevalence of poverty and hunger underscores the importance of a relatively simple life-style and a Christian compassion for people who hurt. Every individual Christian
and every Christian church should have some systematic
way of sharing with the needy and hungry at home and
around the world.

*By this we may be sure that we are in him: he who says
he abides in him ought to walk in the same way in which
he walked* (1 John 2:5-6, author's italics).

*This is how we know we are in him: Whoever claims to live
in him must walk as Jesus did* (1 John 2:5-6, NIV, author's
italics).

If you and I sought seriously to do this, how would it

affect our life-style? Does it concern or scare you to ask that question? I am persuaded that for many of us it would mean a drastically different style of life.

Notes

1. Ronald J. Sider, *Lifestyle in the Eighties* (Philadelphia: Westminster Press, 1982), p. 55.

2. Jacques Ellul, *The Presence of the Kingdom* (London: SCM Press, Ltd., 1951), p. 46.

3. Jim Wallis, *The Call to Conversion* (San Francisco: Harper and Row, Publishers, 1981), pp. 13-14.

4. Ibid., p. 19.

5. Jim Wallis, *Agenda for Biblical People* (New York: Harper and Row, Publishers, 1976), p. 94.

6
He Magnified Service

This chapter will differ somewhat in format from the preceding chapters. There will be only two major divisions or sections: "Service and Greatness" and "Service Demonstrated." These major sections will each be based primarily on the study or interpretation of one particular passage of Scripture. This will entail more specific interpretation than has been true in preceding chapters.

There will be an opening and closing section entitled "Introduction" and "Conclusion." The introduction will include a limited study of the major words translated "service" and "servants" in our English-language Bibles. Also, attention will be given to the need in contemporary churches for an emphasis on service and/or ministry.

The conclusion, similar to a previous chapter or two, will, among other things, list a few quotations related to service or ministry which you may want to analyze and evaluate.

Introduction

Ten or more Greek words are at times translated "service" or "servants." One reason for some hesitation in saying exactly how many Greek words are translated by a certain English word is the large number of translations of the Scriptures that we now have. Naturally, they fre-

quently vary in the translation of words from the original
languages.

There is no doubt about the major words that are translated "service" or "servant." They are *diakonos* and
doulos. The former is predominantly a Pauline word. In
contrast to the eight times it is found in the Gospels, it is
used twenty-one times in the Pauline Epistles. Paul spoke
of himself as a *diakonos* at least five times. If my count is
correct, the word in its various forms (noun, verb, etc.) is
used ninety-two times in the New Testament with forty-
four of those in the Pauline Epistles. The word *diakonos*
evidently came closest to describing what some of the
members of the church did in service to the Christian
fellowship. Hence, in the early church, *diakonos* (deacon)
became the title for certain leaders (Phil. 1:1; 1 Tim. 3:8,
12). A factor of considerable importance in the contemporary discussion of the place of women in the life and struc-
ture of the church is the meaning by Paul when, in the
first verse of the closing chapter of his letter or epistle to
the church at Rome, he used the word in the feminine
form: "I commend to you our sister Phoebe, a deaconess
of the church at Cenchreae" (Rom. 16:1). The translations
vary considerably. Where the Revised Standard Version
says "deaconess," Williams also uses the term *deaconess.*
The *New American Standard Bible,* the New King James
Version, and the *New International Version* say "a servant of the church" while *The Good News Bible* says "who
serves the church." *The New English Bible* describes
Phoebe as a "fellow-Christian who holds office in the congregation."

The other major word translated "servant" is *doulos.* It
is very common in the Gospels, used seventy-three times
especially in Matthew (thirty times) and in Luke (twenty-
seven times) with only eleven times in John's Gospel and

five times in Mark. The word is found very few times in other portions of the New Testament except in the Pauline Epistles (twenty-nine times) and Revelation (fourteen times). Paul, in the introduction to several of his epistles, referred to himself as a servant (*doulos*) of Christ (Rom. 1:1; Gal. 1:10; Phil. 1:1; and Titus 1:1). Incidentally, *doulos* is frequently translated "slave" or "bondservant."

The New Testament perspective, which is seldom specifically formulated, is that men and women are slaves until they become believers. They are then free in Christ. That freedom, however, comes through enslavement to Christ. The question that we can and should ask ourselves is: Whose slave are we—Satan's and sin or Christ's who will increasingly give us the strength to live as He lived?

Peter admonished those to whom he wrote to "live as servants of God" (1 Pet. 2:16). Paul admonished the Galatians, "Through love be servants of one another" (5:13). On one occasion when the disciples had been debating who was the greatest, Jesus said to them, "If any one would be first, he must be last of all and servant of all" (Mark 9:35).

The basic call of God, which is one to every child of His, is to serve or minister. All God's children are called to perform some distinctive service for the Christian fellowship.

An increasing number of churches in recent years have enlarged their programs and as a result have added staff members to care for these additional programs. Any call of God, even to the pastoral ministry, is not a call to some exalted office; rather, it is a call to serve or minister. Furthermore, all of us should remember that as far as our Heavenly Father is concerned, there is no "hierarchy of calling." Even if there were, it would simply mean that the greater responsibility would rest on the ones with the

"highest" calling. Really, the highest call of God is a call
to follow His leading, to do His will. This sense of purpose
or call can be true of those who have not felt a call to
vocational religious service. Those who do not have a
sense of a unique call to vocational religious service can
be just as devoted to the will and purpose of God as those
who have such a call. In other words, the lawyer, the
doctor, the farmer, the politician, the housewife can have,
and many do have, deep convictions of being within the
will of God. They should be just as respected and honored
as any vocational religious worker or even the one who
has been "called to preach."

Along with and to a certain degree a product of the
expanding program of many churches and of church
staffs, an increasing number of young men and young
women have a sense of call to some phase of the Christian
ministry. Some of our churches are struggling with a decision about what they should do regarding these young
people. Should they be ordained? Our churches and
church leaders may be forced, sooner or later, to restudy
the whole matter of New Testament ministry: call and
ordination. If we study the Scriptures with open, sensitive
minds, we may conclude that ordination was a simple
laying on of hands and prayer setting aside an individual
or individuals to a particular task to which God had already set them aside. This certainly seemed to be true of
what the church at Antioch did regarding Paul and Bar-
nabas. For instance, "after fasting and praying they laid
their hands on them and sent them off" (Acts 13:3). Also,
it is possible that a careful analysis of the teachings of the
Scriptures would convince us that there is not set forth in
the New Testament any "orthodox" procedure concerning the recognition of the call and ordination.

It could be helpful to all of us if we would study carefully Paul's sense of God's special call. He had such a sense of call, but he referred to himself as a servant or a slave of Christ. This he did much more frequently than he referred to himself as a preacher. He referred a number of times to his preaching, but he referred only a couple of times to himself as a preacher, both of these in the Pastoral Epistles (1 Tim. 2:7; 2 Tim. 1:11).

We need a fresh study and interpretation of the call of God. If we made a careful study, we might conclude that we and our churches have departed to some degree from the New Testament conception of ministry or service. Let us now examine one of our key passages of Scripture.

Service and Greatness

As we study this section and the following one on "Service Demonstrated," it will be helpful if you will have an open Bible readily available. If you have different versions, which, incidentally, should be true of every serious student of the Scriptures, they should be readily available. At least, it will be helpful if you will keep your Bible, whatever version you may have as your favorite, open as we study together Matthew 20:20-28. Some of you will even find it helpful to have a marker of some kind at Mark 10:35-45. These two accounts are remarkably alike, except the source of the request. In Matthew, it is from the mother of John and James. In Mark, she is not mentioned.

The Request

Matthew says that the mother of John and James "kneeling before him [Jesus] . . . asked him for something" (v. 20) or "begged a favour" (NEB), or made "a request of Him" (NASB). Mark does not mention the mother at all. In Matthew's account, Jesus knew the real source for the

request. He specifically directed his statement to John
and James and not to the mother.

Of particular concern to us in this study is the content
of the request. Jesus asked the mother of John and James
what her request was. Her reply was, "Command that
these two sons of mine may sit, one at your right hand and
one at your left, in your kingdom" (v. 21). These brothers,
with Peter, had been the only ones of the twelve with
Him at the time of His transfiguration and would be the
three who would be with him in the garden of Gethsemane. John was the disciple whom Jesus evidently loved in
a special way. He was the one who "was lying close to the
breast of Jesus" (John 13:23) when they were eating and
Jesus had predicted that one of them was going to betray
Him. To John Jesus entrusted the care of His mother as He
was dying on the cross (John 19:26-27). James, so far as we
know, was the first Christian martyr. It may seem, on the
surface, that their request was a more or less normal expectation. They were simply asking for the two places of
greatest prestige and authority in the Kingdom.

Background for the request. The preceding has set forth
several aspects of the background. Let us fill out the background, at least its general aspects, a little more fully.
Notice the word "then," which, incidentally, is not in
Mark. Although the Gospels are not necessarily chrono-
logical, the first two Synoptic Gospels agree on the immediate background for the request. Jesus and the
disciples were on their way to Jerusalem where Jesus
would be "delivered to the chief priests and scribes, and
they will condemn him to death, . . . to be . . . crucified,
and he will be raised on the third day" (Matt. 20:18-19).

Some writers are generous enough to suggest that possibly John and James were not present when Jesus predicted His crucifixion and resurrection. This seems doubtful.

If they were thinking of what He had said, they evidently concentrated on the fact that "he will be raised on the third day" (v. 19).

It seems that a major recurring topic of conversation and debate among the twelve was which of them would be the greatest in the kingdom which they expected Jesus to establish (Luke 9:46; 22:24; Mark 9:34). They evidently thought in terms of an earthly kingdom. It is hard to believe that all of them expected to be greatest in that kingdom. It could be that the debate was primarily regarding Peter, John, James, and maybe another of the more prominent of the twelve.

It seems that the background for James and John's request was primarily based on what Jesus had said: "When the Son of man shall sit on his glorious throne, you who followed me will also sit on twelve thrones, judging the twelve tribes of Israel" (Matt. 19:28). The latter may have been spoken the same day as what we find in Matthew 20. "Perhaps their minds had been preoccupied with the words of Jesus . . . about their sitting on twelve thrones taking them in a literal sense" (W. P.). Whatever may have been the background for the request, they asked for the places of prestige and power. They were obviously thinking of an earthly physical kingdom instead of a spiritual kingdom. Their request was "for the chief cabinet offices in the new monarchy" (Int. B.). They evidently did not fully understand, as many and possibly most of us in the contemporary period fail to understand, that thrones from God's perspective are associated with suffering.

Response of Jesus to the Request

Jesus "turned to the brothers" (NEB) and replied to the request with a statement and then a question. "You do not know [understand, NEB] what you are asking." It may be, as one commentator suggests, that the words were "spoken in a tone of infinite tenderness and sadness" (Ell.). "Are you able to drink the cup that I am to drink?" (v. 22). They evidently did not understand that if Jesus and the Father were to grant their request it would involve suffering. They had not yet understood "that nearness to Him and His glory could only be attained by equal nearness in suffering" (Ell.). How often could it be said of us that we do not understand what all may be involved in God answering some of the things we request of the Father?

Jesus addressed an additional question to John and James, a question He might ask any of us who desire positions of prestige and power in our church or denomination. "Are you able to drink the cup that I am to drink?" We wonder if they understood the deeper meaning of "the cup" when they replied, "We are able." Did they prove that they were able when Jesus was arrested and led away to be tried and ultimately crucified? However, we should not be too hard on John and James. Would we have shown any more courage and been any more committed than they and the others were if we faced a similar situation?

The "cup" is a metaphor used with two drastically different meanings in the Scriptures. Some references are to the cup of joy (Ps. 16:5; 23:5; 116:13). Here and in several other places reference is made to the cup of sorrow or suffering (Isa. 51:17; Jer. 49:12; Lam. 4:21; Matt. 20:22).

The answer of John and James has been labeled as "amazing proof of their ignorance and self-confidence, ambition had blinded their eyes" (W. P.). Let us not be too hard on James and John. Have we ever faced up to the price we would have to pay if we followed Jesus completely or fully? Have you ever, as I have at times, been gripped with a deep concern if not fear of the price you might have to pay if you did fully what the Father would have you do?

Jesus did tell John and James that they would drink of the cup that he would struggle with in the garden of Gethsemane and drink fully at Calvary. In other words, they would suffer as followers of His. James was one of the first of His followers who paid with their lives for being a Christian (Acts 12:2), possibly preceded only by Stephen. What a debt we owe to James and the other Christian martyrs!

Jesus further said that determining who sat on his right hand and left hand was not His prerogative. Those places were reserved by the Father. The reference could be to particular individuals or more likely individuals who met certain requirements. Whatever it might mean, the decision was not Christ's but the Father's.

Reaction of the Other Disciples

When the ten heard about the request, they were indignant. How did the ten hear about the request? Had it been made in their presence? Doubtlessly not. Had the mother of John and James shared it with one or more of the other disciples? Had John and/or James told one of the ten? There is no way to know how or from whom they had learned of the request. There was no doubt about their reaction, they were indignant.

Why were they so indignant? It could be that their anger stemmed from the fact that John and James had thought of it first, or at least they were the first to approach Jesus directly about a place in His kingdom. After all, the twelve had debated or argued from time to time about who was greatest in the Kingdom. My judgment is that the debate centered around James, John, and Peter

more than about any others. The ten, as well as James and
John, were still thinking in terms of an earthly kingdom.

A factor in the anger of the ten may have been the
feeling among them that John and James were taking
advantage of their family relation to Jesus. Barclay suggested that "James and John were almost certainly full
cousins of Jesus." If this were correct, and it is supported
by some other commentators, then the ten were extremely angry primarily because they felt that James and
John had taken advantage of their family relation to Jesus
in making their request.

How did Jesus react to the reaction of the ten? He
"called them to him," which would suggest that the ten
were not close by and could not have directly heard the
request. There are two or three matters in the statement
of Jesus to the ten that contain significant messages for us,
His contemporary followers. Notice that Jesus did not condemn the desire for greatness. There is nothing wrong
with Christians wanting to be great if they have the right
Christian conception of greatness and if they are willing
to pay the price to obtain that greatness, and the price
may be very high. Here we have the most pointed and
drastically different statement about service as a basis for
greatness. The general judgment of the people of the
world today, as in the days of Jesus, is that the great are
served. In contrast, greatness for Jesus, and should be for
His followers of every age, is that the truly great serve or
minister to others. The word of Jesus was and is: "Whoever would be great among you must be your servant
[*diakonos*], and whoever would be first among you must
be your slave [*doulos*]." This is a complete reversal of the
general or popular opinion in the contemporary world as
well as in biblical days.

✦ *Conclusion*

While it will involve some repetition, it seems wise to set forth a few conclusions we can and should draw from this study of service and greatness. Jesus did not criticize the desire for greatness by His disciples. But for the desire for greatness to be approved by Him, there must be the proper basis for judging greatness. "The world may assess a man's greatness by the number of people he controls; . . . or by his intellectual standing and academic eminence; . . . or by the size of his bank balance and the material possessions which he has amassed" (Bar.). Barclay went on to conclude, "But in the assessment of Jesus Christ these things are irrelevant. His assessment is quite simple—how many people have you helped?"

The idea that true greatness from the Christian perspective is determined by service to people not only applies to individuals but also to churches and even denominations and the agencies and institutions they support. It should be remembered, for example, that the big church or the thriving institution may not be a great church or institution. The greatness of a local church cannot be measured in terms of the buildings that it has, the eloquence of the preacher, the skill of the choir, or the bigness of its budget and offerings.

A small church, with inadequate facilities and leadership that is limited in native ability and training, may be a great church. The great individual child of God and the great church are ones who care and share with people in the church, the community, and the world. Such an individual or church will have a particular concern about people, young and old, who are lonely, who hurt, who are in need of a touch motivated by a compassion that is derived from their vital relation to the compassionate, living Christ.

Service Demonstrated

The major Scripture we will use in this section on the demonstration of service and hence of real greatness will be John 13. This incident of the washing of the disciples' feet is recorded only in John's Gospel. Many insights into the kind of life Jesus lived and the type of person He really was would be missing if we did not have John's Gospel. One of the most significant of these distinctly Johannine insights into the life of Jesus was the washing of the disciples' feet.

This incident is more impressive if we take note of when it was done. There are some differences of opinion about the relation of this supper to the Passover and the trial and crucifixion of Jesus. Generally speaking, however, there is agreement that it was the last night of His earthly life.

The first verse of John 13 is introductory. Note a few things about the verse. This washing of the disciples' feet took place "before the feast of the Passover." This may have been the night before Passover began or it is even possible that the meal that night was the Passover meal followed by the institution of the Lord's Supper (Mark 14:12-23; Matt. 26:21-25; Luke 22:7-23, W. P.). This was a time when Jesus could have been expected to think about Himself. After all, the next day He would be arrested, tried, and crucified. But what does the Scripture say: "When Jesus knew that his hour had come to depart out of this world to the Father." "When" is the background for what He did that night. It could mean "although He knew" or "because He knew." The *Cambridge Bible* says, "The latter is better: it was . . . because He knew that He would soon return to glory that He gave this last token of self-humiliating love." He left them an example of self-denying love.

Paul exhorted the Philippians and would exhort us: "Have this mind among yourselves, which is yours in Christ Jesus, who, though he was in the form of God, did not count equality with God a thing to be grasped, but emptied himself, taking the form of a servant, being born in the likeness of men" (Phil. 2:5-7). No incident in the life of Jesus more pointedly underscored His servant role than when He washed the disciples' feet.

Jesus had loved "his own who were in the world, he loved them to the end" (v. 1). The latter part of this verse evidently does not refer to the end of life. Rather, He loved them "in the highest degree" (Exp. Gr.). His love for them and for us was and is limitless.

This same Jesus expressed the extremity of His love by performing a task that a servant usually performed. In the absence of a servant, one of the disciples should have performed the service. The roads they traveled were dusty or muddy. They were doubtlessly barefooted or at best wore sandals. The dust or mud needed to be washed from their feet. The disciples who debated from time to time about who would be the greatest in the Lord's kingdom would not stoop as low as to perform a task of a slave or a servant.

They were reclining at the table. Their feet extended away from the table.

The incident took place after they were ready for *the* supper. This was not an ordinary meal. The definite article *the* underscores the supper's importance. But after they were all ready for the supper, what did Jesus do? The washing may have be done during the supper, but doubtlessly it was when they were in place and ready for the supper. Such would be out of place during a meal.

Can you visualize what happened? Can you see Jesus rising from the table, girding a towel around Himself, pouring water into *the* basin—a basin provided by the host—and beginning to wash the disciples' feet? We might expect one of them to have jumped to his feet and say, "Not so, Lord, let me wash the feet of the others." But not a man spoke up.

Can you visualize Jesus at the feet of Judas? Jesus knew that Judas was going to betray Him. What a picture! What a lesson for us! My judgment is that there was real tenderness in His touch. It is possible that Jesus did not reveal at that time what Judas was going to do because He may have been concerned about what Peter, the sons of Thunder, and some others might do to Judas.

Wherever Jesus may have started the washing, nothing was heard except the water dripping from the feet into the basin until Jesus reached impetuous Peter. "Lord, do you wash my feet?" (v. 6). The pronouns "you" and "my" stand together in the beginning of Peter's question. This indicated a marked contrast. Then, after Jesus had told Peter, and doubtlessly it was meant for all the disciples, that he did not understand what Jesus was doing but he would understand later, Peter emphatically said, "You shall never wash my feet" (v. 8). "Never" is the translation of a double negative. Can you see Peter drawing his feet up?

Then Jesus talked about inner spiritual cleansing while Peter and doubtlessly the other disciples continued to interpret what Jesus said as references to physical washing. The words of Jesus to Peter were: "If I do not wash you, you have no part in me" (v. 8). Typically, Peter said, "Lord, not my feet only but also my hands and my head!"

(the other exposed parts of his body, v. 9). Jesus said that one who had bathed is clean all over. Then He shifted immediately to spiritual cleansing: "You are clean, but not every one of you" (v. 10). Knowing that Judas was going to betray him, He said, "you are not all clean."

After Jesus washed the feet of the disciples, He resumed His place at the table. Can you imagine the eyes of the disciples fixed on Jesus? He asked them a pointed and challenging question: "Do you know what I have done to you?" (v. 12). Do you really understand? To help them answer His question, He reminded them that they called Him Lord and Teacher and that He had washed their feet. They should be willing to perform the same type of humble service.

How that spirit of unselfish, loving service can and should be expressed from age to age will vary. There are few if any dirty or dusty feet to wash in our day. There are, however, an abundance of people—sometimes they are close by—who need some type of Christian ministry. Many of them need the type of unselfish, loving ministry that Jesus would provide if He were here in person. Now He depends on those who have Him living within them. He wants to express something of His concern and compassion through believers for those who hurt. Jesus said of Himself, "I am among you as one who serves" (Luke 22: 27). Would it not be great if people could say of you and me, "You are among us as one who serves"? We can know that this can be truthfully said of us only to the degree that we let the resurrected Christ live in us and express Himself through us.

And let us never forget: "A servant is not greater than his master" (John 13:16). This statement occurs elsewhere in the Gospels, and each time in a different context (Matt. 10:24; Luke 6:40). Jesus was their Master, and yet he humbled Himself and washed their feet. They were, and we are, servants. Certainly, if He, the Master, performed that type of humble service, we, His disciples, should be willing to exemplify the same kind of life.

They and we are "sent ones." He is the One who sent them and sends us. Jesus had a concluding exhortation to the disciples which should be a continuing challenge to His disciples of every age: "If you know these things, blessed are you if you do them" (v. 17).

Conclusion

When we, as disciples of Jesus, are tempted to avoid any kind of service to God and/or other persons because of our dignity and prestige, let us remember Jesus, the matchless Son of God, with a towel around Him, a basin of water in His hand, washing the disciples' feet.

In his commentary on John's Gospel, William Barclay says that the nearness of Jesus "to God so far from separating Him from man, brought Him nearer than ever to men. It is always true that there is no one closer to men than the man who is close to God." On the other hand, "the nearer we are to suffering humanity, the nearer we are to God."[1]

Barclay also says that in the washing of the feet of the disciples by Jesus "is the lesson and the proof that there is only one kind of greatness, and that is the greatness of service."[2]

Peter said, "Clothe yourselves, all of you, with humility toward one another, 'for God opposes the proud, but gives grace to the humble' " (1 Pet. 5:5). This may sound like a strange statement coming from Peter. But Peter had learned, or at least was in the process of learning, that the truly great Christian men and women are those who will perform the humblest of service or ministry.

> *By this we may be sure that we are in him: he who says*
> *he abides in him ought to walk in the same way in which*
> *he walked* (1 John 2:5-6, author's italics)

> *This is how we may be sure we are in him: he who says he*
> *'remains in him' ought to be living as he lived* (1 John
> 2:5-6, Moffatt, author's italics)

Notes

1. William Barclay, *Gospel of John,* rev. ed. (Philadelphia:
Westminster Press, 1955), p. 160.
   2. Ibid., p. 162.

7

He Was Compassionate

This chapter, like most others, is closely related to preceding and following chapters. For example, the emphasis of the two following chapters comes from the fact that Jesus was and is a compassionate person. His compassion motivated Him to reach out and touch people (chap. 8). His compassion was a factor in the fact that He separated the sinner and His sin—condemning the sin but reaching out in love and compassion to the sinner. Because so much of the life that Jesus lived while He walked among people was an expression of His compassion, we will have to limit our study in this chapter to places where the word *compassion* is actually used.

Even a cursory reading of the Gospels will indicate that the compassion of Christ was not a superficial type of emotion. If we walk as He walked or live as He lived, we will have a similar deep and abiding compassion for people, particularly for people who suffer. That "suffering" may be mental and emotional as well as physical. Compassion that reaches out to people in need is not a superficial emotional experience. But that does not mean that emotions should not be expressed. One of the dangers of advanced education is that it may tend to rob one of real warmth in his or her relations to people. It may be wise for us to remember that Jesus wept over Jerusalem (Luke

113

19:41) and also wept with Mary and her friends (John 11:35). The latter is the shortest verse in the Scriptures, but few have a deeper reach into our lives. Can we and do we weep with those who weep?

Meaning of Compassion

The word *compassion* is derived from two Latin words: *pati* (suffer) and *cum* (with). It means to "suffer with one who suffers."

> Compassion asks us to go where it hurts, to enter into places of pain, to share in brokenness, fear, confusion, and anguish. Compassion challenges us to cry out with those in misery, . . . to weep with those in tears. . . . Compassion means full immersion in the condition of being human. . . . something more is involved than a general kindness or tenderheartedness. It is not surprising that compassion, understood as suffering with, often evokes in us a deep resistance and even protest.[1]

Compassion could be read as "com-patience," since *patience* as well as *suffer* are rooted in the Latin *pate*. This means, among other things, that a compassionate person is one who is patient with others in their condition of life, their weaknesses, and even their sins.

A compassionate person is not one who reaches down to the less privileged. Rather, the compassionate person reaches out. If one reaches down at all, one reaches as a brother or sister who seeks as best he or she can to understand and to enter into the suffering and problems of others, who are real or potential brothers or sisters in Christ.

Sometimes *sympathy* or *pity* are used as synonyms of *compassion.* Some of you, as is true of me, may have some problem equating compassion with pity. If one is not careful, pity can become condescending in spirit and attitude. This is certainly not true of real Christian compassion. Compassion may include pity, but if so it is a pity accompanied with an urge to help those who hurt and with no sense of superiority.

A brief examination of the major Greek word for *compassion* in the New Testament will give us some insight into its meaning. Barclay says that the word refers to

> what are known as the nobler viscera, that is, the heart, the lungs, the liver and the intestines. The Greeks held these to be the seat of the emotions, . . . It is from that idea that the verb *splagchnizesthai* was formed in later Greek. It means *to be moved with compassion,* . . . it describes no ordinary pity or compassion, but an emotion which moves a man to the very depths of his being. It is the strongest word in the Greek for the feeling of compassion.[2]

Barclay also calls attention to the fact that Greeks could not imagine that God, any god, would feel compassion for any human person. For the Greeks, using the word for *compassion* in setting forth the nature of any divine person was unthinkable. The world could not and would not have ever known our God as the God of compassion without the revelation of the Father by the Son, who "reflects the glory of God and bears the very stamp of his nature" (Heb. 1:3). Also, the Gospel writers from time to time refer to the fact that Jesus was "moved with compassion."

Several words are sometimes translated "compassion." The major word, however, is *splagchnai*. The noun is variously translated. The verb form is found twelve times in the Scriptures with all of these references in the Synoptic Gospels. In other words, it is a distinctly Synoptic word. With four exceptions, the verb is translated "compassion" in the Revised Standard Version. The other four times, it is translated "pity" (Matt. 18:27; 20:34; Mark 1:41; 9:22). In all except two occurrences, the reference is to the compassion of Christ. Those exceptions are two of the better-known parables of Jesus: the good Samaritan (Luke 10:33) and the prodigal son (Luke 15:20). The latter could just as appropriately be called the parable of the compassionate father.

The different translations of the New Testament vary from time to time in their translation of Greek words. This is definitely true of the translation of the verb form of the word for *compassion.* For example, the King James Version consistently translates the word "compassion." The other versions of the Scripture vary some. For example, in Matthew 9:36, the King James Version, the *New International Version,* the *New American Standard Bible* and the Revised Standard Version translate the word *compassion* while *The New English Bible* translates it *pity.* There are other variations but none of major importance.

Let us turn now to a relatively few specific references to the compassion of Jesus. We will divide these references into His compassion for the multitude or crowds and His compassion for individuals.

The Compassion of Christ

On more than one occasion, the compassion of Jesus for the restless, moving, hungry masses was recorded. For example, "When he saw the crowds, he had compassion on them because they were harassed and helpless, like sheep without a shepherd" (Matt. 9:36). Then He said to the disciples, and I am persuaded He would say the same to His present-day disciples, "The harvest is plentiful, but the laborers are few; pray therefore the Lord of the harvest to send out laborers into his harvest" (vv. 37-38). We should admit that laborers are not only needed on the mission fields of the world but are also needed in our local communities. We may discover, if and when we pray for laborers to be sent, that He will ask us to help answer our own prayers.

On another occasion, "as he went ashore he saw a great throng; and he had compassion on them, and healed their sick" (Matt. 14:14). This was the background for the feeding of the five thousand, which is recorded in all four Gospels (Matt. 14:13-21; Mark 6:32-44; Luke 9:10-17; John 6:1-13).

On another occasion, Jesus said to the disciples: "I have compassion on the crowd, because they have been with me now three days, and have nothing to eat; and I am unwilling to send them away hungry, lest they faint on the way" (Matt. 15:32). This was the occasion for the miraculous feeding of the four thousand.

Jesus is not here in the flesh today. Will you not agree that He wants us to see the multitude and do what we can about their needs, particularly their deeper needs? Have you seen the crowds in the cities of our nation and the world? We should remember that many of the restless masses are not in the great centers of population. They will be found in the villages and the rural areas of the world. Regardless of where they live, have we seen the marching, restless masses of the world?

The compassion of Jesus is also specifically indicated as the motivation for some of the occasions when He touched individuals and healed them. Compassion is specifically stated as the motive for His healing the eyes of the blind (Matt. 20:34), the healing of the leper (Mark 1:41), and the raising of the son of the widow of Nain (Luke 7:13).

I will not take the space to review the parable of the prodigal son which might properly be called, as suggested earlier, the parable of the compassionate father. When the prodigal came to his senses in a far country, he determined to return to his home and tell his father that he was no longer worthy to be called his son. "But while he was yet at a distance, his father saw him and had compassion, and ran and embraced him and kissed him" (Luke 15:20). All that follows in this beautiful and touching parable is grounded on and expressive of the fact that the father had compassion on the son who had wandered away not only from his home but also, like many "prodigal sons" through the centuries, away from the way of life he had been taught by word of mouth and doubtlessly by demonstration in the life lived by that father.

Nature of the Compassion of Christ

Based on what has been said concerning the compassion of Christ, how can we summarize its nature?

Particularlized as Well as Generalized

Jesus not only had compassion on the crowd or multitude but on individuals as well. Some Christians contend that they love people in general or those of a particular race or culture, but they seem to fail in expressing that love or compassion to individual people in such groups. If we love people of a different ethnic group or color, we should have compassion for individuals in that group. If we do not, then our "love" and "compassion" should be considered at least superficial, if not an actual pretense.

Jesus, at times, seemed to forget the crowd in order to minister to a particular individual in or at the fringe of the crowd. A well-known example of Jesus' interest in and ministry to individuals was the widow of Nain, whose son was brought back to life (Luke 7:11-17). Another example was Zacchaeus, the tax collector. Jesus took the initiative and called to Zacchaeus to come down from the sycamore tree so that He might go home with him. Some of the people complained that Jesus had gone to eat with a sinner (Luke 19:1-10). Another striking example of compassion when Jesus reached out to minister to an individual in the midst of a crowd was when the woman was healed by touching the hem of His garment (Luke 8:43-48). Still another case was the opening of the eyes of a blind man who cried out for help (Luke 18:35-43). ·

✱ *Universalized not Compartmentalized*

Another characteristic of the compassion of Jesus was the fact that it was *universalized not comparmentalized.* Jesus reached out in compassion to all kinds of people. We can believe that Jesus sought to reach out in compassion to the up and outs as well as the down and outs. We know that when a Pharisee opened his door to Jesus He stepped in. Three specific cases in the Gospels mention such invitations. Jesus seemed to have a special concern and compassion for the social and moral outcasts of the society of His day. But Jesus doubtlessly was considered partial to the underprivileged simply because He was impartial.

This seeming partiality was evident in His relation to and concern for the sick and suffering and even for the sinning. I do not believe we can find a single condemnation of a sinner by Jesus, except the self-righteous sinner. This is something that many of us need to remember. The self-righteous spirit is entirely too prevalent among contemporary church members.

Another area where the compassion of Jesus was especially evident was His concern for the deformed in body and the demented in mind. His compassion reached out to anyone who was not considered "normal." If we follow in His train, we will never tell a joke from the pulpit or in private conversation about someone handicapped in body or mind. If such a joke is told, we can be relatively sure if very many people hear it, one or more will be hurt by the joke.

Jesus seemingly had a special concern and compassion for the underprivileged in general. This included women and little children. I believe if He were alive in the flesh today Jesus' special concern would include older adults. Some of our churches, but not enough of them, attempt to have a special ministry to these and other under-privileged or handicapped groups.

We possibly emphasized more in the past than in the contemporary period "a compassion for souls." L. R. Scar-borough was one of the outstanding evangelists of a cou-ple of generations ago. I heard him say to a relatively small group on one occasion, "I can close my eyes night or day and weep over a lost world." His compassion was the major secret of his power as an evangelist. I do not believe that Dr. Scarborough was compartmentalizing people when he spoke of their souls.

It has been too true, however, in the past and to some degree in the present, that some refer to the soul as if it were a separate entity. The compassion of Jesus was for people, period. Will you not agree that if we had more of a concern and compassion for people as such that even our evangelistic results would be greater and of a sounder quality?

Internalized Before Externalized

Another characteristic of the compassion of Christ, which is not so specifically evident as some of the others, is the fact that it was *internalized before it was external-ized*. There was no put on or pretense about Jesus' com-passion. There was no conflict between how He felt

within and what He did. As was true of His life in general
and as is increasingly true of a maturing Christian, life
flowed from within outward.

Expressed in Helpful Ministry

One other characteristic of the compassion of Jesus
which should be true of us as His disciples is the fact that
His compassion always *expressed itself in a helpful ministry.* His compassion was no vaporous concept. It led Him
to come to grips with the real needs of people. For example, He had compassion on the multitude and healed their
sick. He had compassion on the multitude and fed them.
He had compassion for the blind and the leper and healed
them. He had compassion on the widow of Nain and
brought her son back to life.

First John contains a good admonition for all of us: "Little children, let us not love in word or speech but in deed
and in truth" (3:18). We would be wise to remember that,
if the compassion we may have for the hurts and needs of
people is not expressed in some practical ways of ministry,
there will be a tendency for the compassion itself to be
less responsive. In other words, we will become less sensitive to the needs of people.

Conclusion

I will conclude this chapter as I have others, with some
quotations. In most cases, some brief statements will be
made or questions asked that will relate the statements or
questions to our contemporary situation.

Man's Question to God

If I were a pastor, I think I would frequently preach a
series of sermons. If I did, one series I would definitely
want to develop would be: "Questions God Asks People,"

with a companion series on "Questions People Have Asked God."

A casual reading of the first few chapters of Genesis will reveal several questions, particularly questions God asked. "Where are you?" (Gen. 3:9); "What is this that you have done?" (Gen. 3:13); "Where is Abel your brother?" (Gen. 4:9). All of these questions are relevant for us today.

As far as we know, the first question man asked God was Cain's question in response to God's question: "Where is Abel?" Cain's question was, "Am I my brother's keeper?" (Gen. 4:9). Just as the early questions that God asked are abidingly relevant and challenging to us today, likewise, Cain's question has continued to be asked by men and women through the centuries.

God's reply to Cain has been His continuing answer through the centuries. God said—continues to say—that Cain was responsible for his brother; therefore men and women through the centuries have been responsible to God for what they do to their brothers and sisters. We should never forget that "brother" from the Christian perspective ultimately includes human brothers and sisters in general and not exclusively Christian brothers and sisters.

 ### *Wonder of Wonders*

The wonder of wonders of the Christian life is that our salvation in Christ becomes a reality in our lives not because we deserve it. That experience when we become one with Christ, when He comes into our lives to live, is a product of Christ's compassion. Paul expressed some of that wonder when he wrote to the Roman Christians: "Wretched man that I am! Who will deliver me from this body of death?" He answered his own question by writ-

ing, "Thanks be to God through Jesus Christ our Lord!"
(Rom. 7:24-25).

Unbelievable Forgiveness and Compassion

When those who were to crucify Jesus came to the place
which is called "The Skull," they crucified Him and the
criminals, one on the right and one on the left. And Jesus
said, "Father, forgive them; for they know not what they
do" (Luke 23:33-34). Someone has said those words were
"tuned to what His whole life had been expressing, an
infinite compassion." There at Calvary, Love was crucified. But that crucifixion was accepted and not rejected,
and hence it became redemptive.

"Points the Way"

Samuel Dresner said, "The compassion of God points
the 'way' for man, for when a man acts compassionately,
he is walking in the 'way' of the Lord. This is the meaning
of *imitatio Dei.*" If judged by our compassion for people,
how much of the image of God do folk see revealed in us?

Proclamation and Demonstration

Jim Wallis suggested that the quality of life in the early
Christian community was a vital part of the evangelistic
outreach of the early church.

> Christian fellowship became the companion of the Chris-
> tian gospel; demonstration was vitally linked to proclama-
> tion. The oneness of word and deed, . . . lent power and
> force to the witness of the early Christians. . . . The word
> was not only announced but seen in the community of
> those who were giving it flesh.[3]

How thoroughly is the Christian message demonstrated

in our lives and in the life and fellowship of your church and mine?

A Radical Call

McNeill, Morrison, and Nouwen frequently emphasize the radical nature of the call to be compassionate. "It is a call that goes right against the grain; that turns us completely around and requires a total conversion of heart and mind. It is indeed a radical call, a call that goes to the roots of our lives."[4] They suggest that we as Christians "are called to be compassionate as our Father is compassionate. In and through him, it becomes possible to be effective witnesses to God's compassion and to be signs of hope in the midst of a despairing world."[5] The same authors also suggest that "the great call we have heard is to live a compassionate life."[6] How clearly have we heard that call? What is more important, what has been our response to that call?

Effective Compassion

The effectiveness of our compassion will be determined, to a considerable degree, by the experiences we have had when family and friends have been compassionate in relation to us. Our effectiveness will also be determined by our reactions to the conditions in our lives that called forth compassion from others and the way we responded to their compassion.

Edwin McNeill Poteat, whom I knew personally in my college days, has four lines in a poem of his that somewhat express the preceding idea:

> He cannot heal who has not suffered much,
> For only sorrow sorrow understands;
> They will not come for healing at our touch,
> Who have not seen the scars upon our hands.

✱ Some Searching Questions

Samuel Dresner asks some questions that all of us should be willing to ask and seek to answer honestly. Do we know something of the pain of our friends when they pour out their woes to us, or do we listen with cold hearts? "Do we offer a helping hand to the needy relative, or do we go out of our way to avoid meeting him?" "Do we assist the blind to cross the street, or do we hurry on, confident that someone else will do it?"[7]

✱ A Challenging Scripture

"What does it profit . . . if a man says he has faith and has not works? Can his faith save him? If a brother or sister is ill-clad and in lack of daily food, and one of you says to them, 'Go in peace, be warmed and filled,' without giving them the things needed for the body, what does it profit? So faith by itself, if it has no works, is dead" (Jas. 2:14-17).

Will you not agree that entirely too many Christians who claim to be compassionate do little if anything to help the hungry and suffering?

✱ Great Christians

The spiritual stature of a child of God cannot be judged by the position he holds or what people think of him. The greatness of a child of God can be correctly measured only when compared to the stature or greatness of Jesus, who fully revealed the Father. In other words, how much is he or she like Jesus in his or her attitude toward and relation to people?

Sometimes the really great are generally recognized. This was true of David Brainerd who died of tuberculosis while ministering to the Indians, true of Billy Graham, and many more. But let us never forget that many of God's great people are among the little people of the world, rarely known outside of a very limited group of relatives and friends.

Compassion Demonstrated

My family and I have had the privilege of visiting several mission fields. The most striking examples that we have seen of Christian compassion have been by some missionary friends. They have left family, friends, and their native land to share the gospel with other people. On one occasion we were in Beirut, Lebanon, for several weeks. An unforgetable experience to my wife was a visit with two relatively young women to a mission in a refugee camp. These cultured, refined single women had had considerable mistreatment by some of the Palestinians in the camp. This included the throwing of cow dung at them. Nothing, however, kept them from going regularly for the services in the chapel. I won't give their names. One is dead now. It might be an embarrassment to the other.

On another occasion, we were in Sao Paulo, Brazil, one of the most rapidly growing cities in the world. We had seen the evidences of the prosperity of the city, but we wanted to see where some of the extremely poor people lived. As is typical of much of Latin America, the slums were on the hills and mountains which would have been the area where the well-to-do might live in our country.

A veteran missionary took us on a trip that we shall never forget. It was definitely a slum area. There was no provision to care for the sewage. It ran down shallow ditches. Most of the people lived in little shacks they had built themselves from scraps of wood and tin. We went into one of those homes where there was a young baby. During the visit in the home, the cultured, well-educated missionary took that baby in her arms and cuddled it. She seemed oblivious to the dirt and possible germs.

These are only two of many possible illustrations of compassion by missionary men and women.

By this we may be sure that we are in him: he who says he abides in him ought to walk in the same way in which he walked (1 John 2:5-6, author's italics)

This is how we can be sure that we are in union with God: whoever says that he remains in union with God should live just as Jesus Christ did (1 John 2:5-6, GNB, author's italics)

How much does the compassion of Christ find expression in and through your life and mine?

Notes

1. Donald P. McNeill, Douglas A. Morrison, and Henri J. M. Nouwen, *Compassion: A Reflection on the Christian Life* (Garden City, N. Y.: Doubleday and Co., Inc., 1982), p. 4.

2. William Barclay, *More New Testament Words* (London: SCM Press, 1958), p. 156.

3. Jim Wallis, *The Call to Conversion* (San Francisco: Harper and Row, Publishers, 1981), p. 15.

4. McNeill, Morrison, and Nouwen, p. 8.

5. Ibid., p. 45.

6. Ibid., p. 133.

7. Samuel H. Dresner, *Prayer, Humility, and Compassion* (Philadelphia: Jewish Publication Society of America, 1957), p. 191.

8

He Touched People

As an expression of concern and compassion, Jesus, as He went about doing good, reached out and touched people. The fact that Jesus' touch is mentioned so frequently in the Bible suggests that there must have been something uniquely tender about His touch.

The walk of Jesus as He lived among people was not an aimless walk. He was more or less constantly touching people, and they were conscious of that touch. Do we need to emphasize again that as Jesus' followers, our walk or lives should not be aimless? We who have been brought into union with the resurrected Christ should be so responsive to His touch on our lives that naturally and inevitably we will unconsciously seek to live the kind of life He lived. We will permit Him, more and more, to touch the lives of others through our touch with and on them. Also, "others" will be constantly enlarging, including family, friends, neighbors, church members, casual acquaintances, and total strangers.

We will tend increasingly to be aware of special concerns for those who in a particular way need a touch by someone who genuinely cares—those will include, among others, those of different classes, colors, and cultures. In other words, the indwelling, compassionate Christ, if we are responsive to Him, will increasingly motivate us to reach out, in a special way, to those who hurt.

Our desire to reach out and touch others will result from our consciousness that we have been touched by Christ. In other words, the more conscious we are of a fresh touch from Jesus, the stronger will be our desire and willingness to touch and minister to others. Few things will reveal more fully and accurately the vitality of our relation to Jesus Christ than how much and meaningfully we touch the lives of all kinds of people, particularly people who are hurting.

The New Testament word, *haptomai* is always translated "touch" in the King James Version. It is a distinctly Synoptic word, being found thirty-one times in the Synoptic Gospels and only once in John's Gospel (John 20:17), once in 1 John (5:18), and three times in the Pauline Epistles (1 Cor. 7:1; 2 Cor. 6:17; Col. 2:21). On all the occasions when this word is found in the Synoptics, it refers to Jesus touching people or people touching Him. Eighteen times the word is used in the Gospels to refer to people touching Jesus and thirteen to the fact that Jesus touched people. However, the former refers to only five distinct incidents, while the latter refers to ten incidents when Jesus touched people.

Early in his Gospel, Luke said, "A great multitude of people . . . came to hear him and to be healed of their diseases; . . . And all the crowd sought to touch him, for power came forth from him and healed them all" (6:17-19).

Mark somewhat succinctly said that "wherever he came, in villages, cities, or country, they laid the sick in the market places, and besought him that they might touch even the fringe of his garment; and as many as touched it were made well" (Mark 6:56; see Matt. 14:34-36).

All three Synoptics report the incident of the woman "who had a flow of blood for twelve years and could not be healed by anyone" (Luke 8:43; see Matt. 9:20; Mark 5:25), who "came up behind him, and touched the fringe of his garment; and immediately her flow of blood ceased" (Luke 8:44). I have told students and young people through the years that they could never fully appreciate the Scriptures unless they had a "holy imagination" that would enable them to visualize the situation and fill in some of the details. Where do you suppose this woman had heard about Jesus' power to heal? Had she had a loved one or a friend who had been healed? There had to be some background for her faith that He could heal her. Notice that she, as was generally true of the multitudes, did not ask Him to touch her. She, like they, sought only to touch the fringe of His garment.

But with that touch, she was healed immediately. Then Jesus asked the question: "Who was it that touched me?" Peter and the other disciples said, "Master, the multitudes surround you and press upon you!" In other words, He was being touched on every side. How did He know about the woman? He answered their query when He said, "Some one touched me; for I perceive that power has gone forth from me" (Luke 8:46). People could not be healed by the touch of Jesus or by touching Him without Him paying a price for that healing. It seems that we, the followers of Jesus, will have a healing influence in the lives of people only to the degree that we pay a price for that ministry.

He Touched to Assure

This may have been the reason for Jesus' touch on other occasions, but it is specifically true in the case of Peter, James, and John on the mount of transfiguration (Matt. 17:1-17; Mark 9:2-13; Luke 9:28-36). The experience on the mount followed by six (eight, according to Luke) days the conversation Jesus had had with His disciples at Caesarea Philippi about six months before His crucifixion. He had given them a test or an examination to see if they understood the kind of Messiah He had come to be.

From that background, Peter, John, and James saw Jesus transfigured, when "his face shone like the sun, and his garments became white as light" (Matt. 17:2). These three disciples heard Moses, representing the Law, and Elijah, representing the prophets, talking to Jesus. Typical of impetuous Peter, he spoke out and said to Jesus: "Lord, it is well that we are here; if you wish, I will make three booths here, one for you and one for Moses and one for Elijah" (v. 4). He was interrupted, and they were overshadowed by a bright cloud. From the cloud came the words: "This is my beloved Son, with whom I am well pleased; listen to him" (v. 5). Those last three words would be good for all of us as God's children to hear: "Listen to him."

The three disciples fell on their faces. Then the assuring touch, "But Jesus came and touched them, saying, 'Rise, and have no fear' And when they lifted up their eyes, they saw no one but Jesus only" (vv. 7-8).

You and I, from time to time, are in need of a touch of assurance. Also, we and many around us may need to hear, "Have no fear."

He Touched to Bless

Every touch of Jesus blessed in some way. But there were incidents where "to bless" was evidently the primary purpose of the touch. This was particularly true of children. "They were bringing children [even infants, Luke] to him, that he might touch them; And he took them in his arms and blessed them, laying his hands upon them" (Mark 10:13,16; see also Matt. 19:13-15; Luke 18: 15-17).

Can you imagine the blessing that the touch of Jesus must have brought to many a youngster and many a home? I can imagine a father or a mother saying to a maturing youngster, "Jesus was here one day in our village, and He took you in his arms and blessed you," or "He laid His hands on your head and pronounced a blessing on you."

Was there a touch on your life in the past that still lingers with you to bless? It may have been the touch of a member of your family or a teacher, a pastor or a friend.

Let me share a personal experience with you. My home was on a farm approximately thirty miles from my college campus. As I started to catch the train back to the campus, I went by the barn to tell my daddy good-bye. He met me under the giant oak tree that stood close to the corner of the barn.

He laid his big, rugged left hand on my shoulder as we shook hands and said good-bye. I can still feel the imprint of that touch. He said something that I have never forgotten, although I am not sure I understood or even now understand what he meant. His closing admonition to me was: "My boy, don't let them take your power away from you up there."

I concluded many years ago that my sharecropper daddy, with his limited formal education, recognized a real danger in education. The danger is that one will tend to substitute one's education for the touch and leadership of the Divine Spirit.

Whether or not Dad's words have been rightly interpreted, you can at least understand why I have never forgotten his touch and the words that were spoken with that touch. You can also understand why I have gone by on occasions when I have been in that general area to see if the giant oak is still standing. It was the last time I was over that way.

Have you had a touch somewhat similar to my experience? More importantly: When have you and I helpfully touched someone—a boy or a girl, a youth, a mature man or woman, or an older person? Have we been and are we channels for the touch of Jesus on the lives of people around us?

He Touched to Heal

Richard C. Trench, in his old but standard book *Notes on the Miracles of Jesus,*[1] listed thirty-three specific miracles performed by or related to Jesus. Practically all of them were performed to meet some human need. Over twenty of them were miracles of healing.

In some miracles, the word *touch* was not used, but it was involved. An example would be Jesus' healing of Peter's mother-in-law. Jesus took her by the hand, and the fever left her. Then there was the striking case of the daughter of Jairus when "taking her by the hand" Jesus "called, saying, 'Child, arise.' And her spirit returned, and she got up at once" (Luke 8:54-56).[2] There is at least one recorded incident when Jesus healed many by laying His hands on them (Luke 4:40). "Laying on" involves or is simply another way of saying touching.

There are several miracles recorded where touching by Jesus was not only not mentioned but where it would have been impossible. Some of these were among Jesus' most striking miracles. One such miracle was the healing of the centurion's servant or slave (Luke 7:1-10; Matt. 8:5-13).

Another similar miracle was the healing or cleansing of the lepers which is recorded only by Doctor Luke (Luke 17:11-19). When the lepers requested that He heal them, Jesus simply told them to go and show themselves to the priests. "And as they went they were healed." Their healing, even while they were on their way to the priests, was proof of their faith in Jesus.

On several occasions, the Bible specifically says that Jesus touched to heal. There were doubtlessly other occasions not mentioned in the Scriptures. When we read reports of Jesus' miracles in the Gospels, as well as other aspects of His ministry and teachings, we should remember what John said: "Now Jesus did many other signs in the presence of the disciples, which were not written in this book; but these are written that you may believe that Jesus is the Christ, the Son of God, and that believing you may have life in his name" (John 20:30-31; see John 21:25).

It would take considerable space to discuss all of the miracles of healing when Jesus touched and healed. I will list these with the places in the Gospels where they are recorded. Regarding some, I will make some brief statements or/and ask some questions. This entire section on the fact that Jesus touched to heal will close with two questions: Why did He touch them? Where did He touch them?

First, miracles that involved the touch of Jesus that are recorded in all three Synoptic Gospels. You may be interested in comparing the accounts in Matthew, Mark, and Luke. You will discover some differences, but none

change their basic thrust. You will also find that the differences are largely, although not exclusively, unimportant.
If the Gospels were all exactly the same, there would be
no reason for three of them. If you have a harmony of the
Gospels, it will make the comparison somewhat simpler.

An example of some variation in all the Synoptics is the
case of the cleansing or healing of the Gerasene demoniac
(Matt. 8:28-34; Mark 5:1-20; Luke 8:26-39).

The healing of the woman with an issue of blood, referred to earlier, is also recorded in all of the Synoptic
Gospels (Matt. 9:20-22; Mark 5:25-34; Luke 8:43-48).

Other miracles involving the touch of Jesus recorded in
all of the Synoptics are: the man with a withered hand
(Matt. 12:9-13; Mark 3:1-5; Luke 6:6-11); the healing of a
"lunatic" (KJV) or epileptic child (Matt. 17:14-21; Mark
9:14-29: Luke 9:37-43), with Mark's record a little fuller in
the description of the boy.

Another striking case is the healing of Bartimaeus, a
blind beggar (Matt. 20:29-34; Mark 10:46-52; Luke 18:35-
43), whose name is mentioned only by Mark. For the
contemporary followers of Jesus, one of the most important truths or lessons for us to get from this particular
incident, as well as from several comparable incidents, is
the fact that Jesus separated the individual from the
masses. He could and frequently did turn from or leave
a crowd to minister to an individual who had a particular
need. This is something that ministers, church staffs, dea-
cons, and ordinary church members find difficult to do.
Also, most of us need to develop a capacity to serve when
people are in need and to be willing to give the time and
energy required to stop and, once knowing their needs,
to do what we can to relieve or supply those needs.

Notice in this incident the place and importance of faith
in the healing process. The word of Jesus was, "Your faith

has made you well." Matthew alone tells us that the healing involved the touch of Jesus. But whether or not Jesus touched those He healed, there was no healing without faith on their part. The word of Jesus to the blind man was: "Receive your sight; your faith has made you well" (Luke 18:42).

Then, what a natural reaction of blind Bartimaeus! When through his faith his sight was restored, he followed Jesus. When we consider the blessings we have received because we are children of God, our response likewise should be a faithful following of the One through whom those blessings have come.

Each of the Synoptic Gospels mentions one or more of the healing miracles not recorded elsewhere. For example, Matthew records the opening of the eyes of two blind men (9:27-31). If you will check the reference, you will discover that "faith" is prominent in the record. Mark also records two miracles that involved the touch of Jesus: "A man who was deaf and had an impediment in his speech." Notice that Jesus "put his fingers into his ears, and he spat and touched his tongue" (7:31-35). Another incident recorded only in Mark is the healing of a blind man (8:22-25). This is one case where Jesus touched the man the second time.

Three miracles are peculiar to Luke. One of these was a woman who was "bent over and could not fully straighten herself" (13:10-17). This miracle had an unusual element. Jesus took the initiative. "He called her and said to her, 'Woman, you are freed from your infirmity.' " Then he laid his hands on her, and she was immediately healed. This was done on the sabbath day which got Jesus into trouble with the ruler of the synagogue.

Luke also records the healing of the man with dropsy ("whose legs and arms were swollen," GNB). While the word *touch* is not found in the record, it does say, "He took him and healed him," which implies that Jesus touched him (14:1-6).

Another miracle recorded only in Luke reveals much about the spirit and compassion of Jesus. When the mob came out to arrest Jesus, one of His disciples took a sword and struck the slave of the high priest and cut off his ear. We know from John's account that Peter struck the slave, the one we would suspect. Luke, the doctor, is the only Gospel writer who said, "But Jesus said, 'No more of this!' And he touched his ear and healed him" (22:51). Don't you wonder about the attitude of Malchus toward Jesus after that?

Two Questions

Two questions were asked earlier: Where did Jesus touch people to heal them? Why did he touch them? The first of these questions relates most specifically to the ones healed. The second question relates to Jesus' touching people in general.

We know where He touched some He healed. He touched them where the healing was needed: the tongue of the one with a speech impediment, the ear of the deaf, the eyes of the blind, and so forth. But where did He touch the leper, one who was considered unclean and avoided by people in general?

The approach of at least one leper is recorded in all of the Synoptic Gospels (Matt. 8:2-4; Mark 1:40-44; Luke 5:12-14). Luke says that, when Jesus was in one of their cities, "there came a man full of leprosy" who "besought him, 'Lord, if you will, you can make me clean.' And [Jesus] stretched out his hand, and touched him, saying, 'I will; be clean.' And immediately the leprosy left him." Where do you think Jesus touched him? We do not know for sure, but my judgment is that He touched him where the leprosy was clearly evident.

In a relatively old but excellent brief book, J. B. Chapman says:

> Anyone would draw away from any attempt of a leper to reach and touch him, but Jesus reached out His hand on purpose and touched the leper. The fountain of purity in Christ was so much fuller than the fountain of impurity in the leper that instead of Jesus' becoming defiled, the leper was made clean. There is cleansing in His touch.[3]

Now, a question that we need to answer and see the application of the answer to our own lives is: Why did Jesus reach out and touch people not only to heal but to bless in general? Will you not agree that Jesus may have touched some people to strengthen their faith? There is no substitute for a touch that is motivated by love and compassion. Mere words are a poor and inadequate substitute.

But will you also agree that Jesus touched some people simply because He wanted to do so? The touch was a natural and normal expression of the way He felt about people, particularly the lonely and those who hurt physically, emotionally, and spiritually. No incident in His walk among people illustrates this concern and compassion more than the raising of the son of the widow of Nain. Several characteristics of Jesus are underscored by this incident which is recorded only in Luke's Gospel (7:11-16). "His disciples and a great crowd went with him." When He and the crowd with Him "drew near to the gate of the city, behold, a man who had died was being carried out, the only son of his mother, and she was a widow." When He saw her, "he had compassion on her and said to her, 'Do not weep.' And He came and touched the bier

[coffin, NASB], and the bearers stood still. And he said,
'Young man, I say to you, arise.' . . . And he gave him to
his mother."

Conclusion

The following are more or less closely related to the fact
that Jesus touched people:

Continuing Need

Chapman suggested that

the touch of Jesus makes all the difference in the world.
We all need our ears touched that we may hear the voice
of God. We need our eyes opened that we may see with
clear vision. We need His touch upon our fevered spirits
that we may have rest. We need His touch upon our hearts
that they may be made clean. We need His touch of assurance that we may not fear in the gathering clouds—clouds
of either sorrow or glory.[4]

An Example

I visited a retired minister and his wife rather regularly.
He was in poor health. When I got ready to leave, he
would call his wife in for a "word of prayer" before I left.
We would either stand with our arms around one another
or hold hands. People like to be touched. This is particularly true of people who are old and ill.

A Touch that Changes Things

The cross was a thing of shame, a way of death reserved
for the worst of criminals. But think what happened to the
cross by the touch of Jesus. It became the outstanding
symbol of the love of God. We now sing: "When I survey
the wondrous cross,/On which the Prince of glory died"
and "In the cross of Christ I glory." What has made the

difference? The touch of the Master. "Wheresoever, whomsoever, whatsoever Jesus touched was changed, enobled, and glorified."

Alice Freeman Palmer suggested years ago, "It is people that count, you want to put yourself into people; they touch other people; these others still, and so you go on working forever."

A Tug

On one occasion when I had spoken to a community group of parents of retarded children on "God and Human Suffering," I was asked to meet some of the children in an adjoining room. The children varied in age and type of handicap. I found myself shortly with each arm around a retarded or handicapped youngster.

This experience helped me to understand more clearly why Jesus healed many people. I think I am honest when I say that I would have given an arm if I could have healed that retarded boy on my left or the retarded girl on my right.

A Testimony

Like you, I can testify concerning the touch of Jesus on my life. On one occasion, I judge I was as near to death as one can go and come back to live. I felt I was given the option to live or die. It would require too much space to tell the whole story. He touched me and brought me back to live. That consciousness gave me a deepened sense of purpose.

The above was a physical touch with deep spiritual overtones. Those overtones went back to an earlier experience when as a teenager I opened my life to the resurrected Christ and was touched by Him. I can visualize where I was when the thought came to me, *These two days with Jesus have meant more to me than all the preceding days of my life.*

Some Questions

I assume that you have been touched by Jesus. Do you feel the need for a fresh touch by Him? What can you do to make a fresh touch more likely to occur?

Are there members of your family and friends of yours who need to be touched by Jesus? Are you willing to be an instrument of Jesus' in touching them?

Will you join with me in confessing that we have not kept the touch of Jesus as fresh and vibrant as it should and can be?

Will you also confess with me that you have not been as consistent as you should have been in sharing Jesus' touch with others?

Will you join with me in a commitment and covenant to be more accessible and seek to be more effective channels for the touch of Jesus on the lives of members of our families, friends, neighbors, and even casual acquaintances and total strangers?

A Poem with a Message

THE TOUCH OF THE MASTER'S HAND

'Twas battered and scarred, and the auctioneer
Thought it scarcely worth his while
To waste much time on the old violin,
But held it up with a smile:
"What am I bidden, good folks," he cried,
"Who'll start the bidding for me?"
"A dollar, a dollar," then, "Two! Only two?
Two dollars, and who'll make it three?
Three dollars once; three dollars, twice,
Going for three—" But no,

From the room, far back, a gray-haired man
Came forward and picked up the bow;
Then, wiping the dust from the old violin,
And tightening the loose strings,
He played a melody pure and sweet
As a caroling angel sings.

The music ceased, and the auctioneer,
With a voice that was quiet and low,
Said: "What am I bid for the old violin?"
And he held it up with the bow.
"A thousand dollars, and who'll make it two?
Two thousand! And who'll make it three?
Three thousand, once, three thousand, twice,
And going, and gone," said he.
The people cheered, but some of them cried,
"We do not understand
What changed its worth." Swift came the reply:
"The touch of a master's hand."

And many a man with life out of tune,
And battered and scarred with sin,
Is auctioned cheap to the thoughtless crowd,
Much like the old violin.
A "mess of pottage," a glass of wine;
A game—and he travels on.
He is "going" once, and "going" twice,
He's "going" and almost "gone."
But the Master comes, and the foolish crowd
Never can quite understand
The worth of a soul and the change that's wrought
By the touch of the Master's hand.[5]

*By this we may be sure that we are in him: he who says
he abides in him ought to walk in the same way in which
he walked* (1 John 2:5-6, author's italics).

By this we can be sure that we are in union with Him:

*Whoever claims, "I am always in union with Him," ought
to live as he lived* (1 John 2:5-6, Williams, author's italics).

How much of the touch of Jesus do we have as we come
into contact with people who need a touch from Him?
When have we touched someone for Him?

Notes

1. Richard C. Trench, *Notes on the Miracles of Jesus* (New
York: Macmillan Co., 1870).

2. Because Luke was a physician, I will use Luke's account of
most cases of healing.

3. J. B. Chapman, *The Touch of Jesus* (Kansas City: Beacon
Hill Press, n. d.), p. 11.

4. Ibid.

5. Myra Brooks Welch, "The Touch of the Master's Hand,"
The Best Loved Poems of the American People, Hazel Felleman,
ed. (Garden City, N. Y.: Doubleday and Company, 1936), pp.
222-223.

9

He Separated the Sinner and His Sin

As Jesus went about doing good, He demonstrated again and again His capacity to separate the sinners and the sin. He reached out in love and compassion for the sinner but disapproved the sin. This is one of the areas where most of us who are disciples find it difficult to follow our Master's example. We find it extremely difficult to separate the sinner and the sin. If we condemn the sin, we seem more or less inevitably to condemn and reject the sinner. Also, most of us tend to grade sins. The worse the sin from our perspective, the stronger is our condemnation of the sinner. Unfortunately, this attitude is so prevalent in many of our churches that ones guilty of certain sins or offenses are not welcome, or at least feel that they are not welcome to come to our church services.

This inability to separate the sinner and the sin helps to explain the fact that many and possibly most of our churches are not reaching more of the unsaved and unenlisted in our communities. In some cases, they may be formally welcomed, but there may be lacking the real warmth that is the product and evidence of a genuine love and compassion for these people in general.

Even a casual examination of the life lived by Jesus proves that the only sinner condemned by Him was the self-righteous sinner. A further examination of Jesus' life

145

indicates that such condemnation was not total or final. This was even true of the Pharisees, the most self-righteous group in the days of Jesus. The fact that Jesus reserved His strongest condemnation for the self-righteous sinner should make some of His contemporary followers uncomfortable. At least, we should ask the following question and seek, as best we can, to answer it honestly: How much are we affected by the self-righteous spirit?

Unfortunately, we who are in the family of God may tend to forget that we are not only sinners "saved by grace" but that we are still sinners. Our sins, in the main, may not be the sins that are generally disapproved by fellow Christians and by society at large. Nevertheless, we know that we have fallen far short of being the kind of person we should be for our Lord. Some of our sins, sins that can handicap and defeat us, are secret sins that, as far as we know, no one else knows about except our Heavenly Father.

In the truest sense, we are in the process of being saved from the power and enslavement of sin. Our salvation from the enslavement of sin will not be complete and final until the end of life's journey when we shall awake in Jesus' likeness. The consciousness of this should give us a deeper understanding of and a genuine compassion for people, regardless of the sins they have committed or are committing.

Associated with Publicans and Sinners

The self-righteous sinners whom Jesus condemned most strongly and pointedly were the Pharisees. We also recognize, however, that Jesus went into the homes of Pharisees when He was invited. At least one prominent Pharisee, Nicodemus, became a secret believer in Jesus as the promised Messiah. He came to Jesus by night. They had a considerable conversation (John 3:1-15), which is the immediate background for the "little gospel"—John 3:16. Nicodemus and Joseph of Arimathea, a secret disciple of Jesus, prepared the body of Jesus for burial and placed it in the new tomb of Joseph (John 19:38-42).

For a complete picture of Jesus' attitude toward, and His relation to sinners, attention should be called to the cleansing of the Temple. He drove out the money-changers and "all who sold and bought in the temple" (Matt. 21:12-13; Mark 11:15-17; Luke 19:45-46). He said to them, "Is it not written. 'My house shall be called a house of prayer for all nations?' But you have made it a den of robbers" (Mark 11:17).

Our interest is in the fact that Jesus associated with publicans and sinners, among the most despised people by the Jews of His day. Who were these two groups? The publicans were the tax collectors who worked for Rome. The sinners might have been any who were not identified with one of the recognized religious groups of that time. In general, they were nonpracticing Jews who were careless about the scribal laws. They were looked down on and avoided by faithful Jews. But Jesus judged people as individuals and not by what group or classification to which they might belong. This was particularly evident in Jesus' attitude toward and relation to the publicans and sinners.

Jesus even took the initiative and invited Himself to the home of Zacchaeus, a chief tax collector who was rich (Luke 19:5). The Jews murmured, saying, "He has gone in to be the guest of a man who is a sinner" (Luke 19:7). How terrible that was! But let us not be too sure that some church members today would not have a similar reaction if their pastor or some leading member of their church went in to have a meal with some of our contemporary "publicans and sinners," the outcasts of our society. And do not be too sure that some such complaints might not come from some of the "leading members" of our churches. What has been and what would be your reaction if such an incident would happen in your church or community?

Let us never forget that because Jesus turned aside to visit with Zacchaeus, salvation came to that house. After all, as Jesus said at the close of the visit in the house of Zacchaeus, "For the Son of man came to seek and to save the lost" (Luke 19:10). In the light of the emphasis of this book, notice that part of the evidence that Zacchaeus had become a new creation was his statement: "Behold, Lord, the half of my goods I give to the poor; and if I have defrauded any one of anything, I restore it fourfold" (Luke 19:8). Wallis said, "He sought to restore justice to those he had wronged in the exercise of his occupation." We should never forget that we cannot be right with God without being right with our fellow human beings.

Luke, on one occasion, said that, when tax collectors and sinners were drawing near to hear Jesus, the Pharisees and scribes murmured, saying, "This man receives sinners and eats with them" (Luke 15:1-2). "If the Gospel of Luke comprised only this one chapter, it would still be precious beyond all estimate; for here, to a degree hardly equalled in any other passage, one feels close to the divine compassion made known through Christ."[1] In Luke's record, this is the immediate background for three of the outstanding parables of Jesus: the lost sheep, the lost coin, and the lost or prodigal son (Luke 15:3-32).

On another occasion after Matthew had responded to the invitation of Jesus to follow Him, many tax collectors and sinners came to a "banquet" Matthew gave for Jesus. When the Pharisees saw that Jesus and His disciples sat with the publicans and sinners, they complained. Jesus responded to their complaint or criticism by saying,

"Those who are well have no need of a physician, but those who are sick. . . . I came not to call the righteous, but sinners" (Matt. 9:10-13). Really, who were the chief sinners who were there that day? Will you agree they were the Pharisees? Let us beware!

Individual Cases

Zacchaeus

Possibly enough attention has been given to the visit that Jesus had in the home of Zacchaeus (Luke 19:1-10). There are few, if any, more adequate illustrations of the fact that Jesus separated the sinner and the sin. Zacchaeus's confession in the presence of Jesus implied that as a tax collector he had wrongfully taken tax money from the people. But Jesus would never permit any sin to keep Him from reaching out to the sinner in compassion and concern.

At least three other cases or examples show the attitude of Jesus toward and His relation to a generally recognized sinner, and here *sinner* is used in the more generally accepted sense. I will trust you to remember most of the details of the incidents or refresh your memory by reading the records of each case.

A Woman of the Street

Jesus accepted an invitation from Simon, the Pharisee, to eat with him. This is one of the three occasions when Jesus accepted an invitation to eat with a Pharisee. All three occasions are recorded in Luke's Gospel (Luke 7:36; 11:37; and 14:1). Luke "is the Gospel of Hospitality." While Jesus was reclining at the table with His sandals removed and His feet stretched out, a woman of the street

—a harlot who doubtlessly had changed her way of life and had repented—wanted to show her gratitude to Jesus.

When the woman stood or knelt at Jesus' feet, she was overcome with emotion. Her tears substituted for the ointment she had brought; she wiped His feet with her hair and kissed and anointed them with the ointment she had brought. After some words to Simon, the Pharisee, Jesus said to the woman, "Your sins are forgiven. . . . Your faith has saved you; go in peace" (Luke 7:48-50). Can you imagine the continuing gratitude of that woman as she reviewed that experience? What, for some of us, may be a more probing question: What is our personal attitude, and what is the predominant attitude in our church, toward those who have sinned and repented of their sins? Is our final word, "Your faith has saved you; go in peace"? Would a woman such as this woman be welcomed into the fellowship of your church and mine?

The Woman Caught in the Act of Adultery

Another specific case when Jesus clearly separated the sinner and the sin was the occasion when the woman caught in the act of adultery was brought into the presence of Jesus by some scribes and Pharisees. This incident is not found in some of the oldest and best manuscripts. Different translations treat it differently. The opinion of many and possibly most New Testament scholars is that the incident really occurred. Surely you and I agree that it is typical of the spirit of Jesus. It clearly revealed Jesus' inclination and capacity to separate the sinner and the sin.

The scribes and Pharisees reminded Jesus of the teachings of the law which would require that the woman be stoned to death. What would He say should be done about her? As usual, they were attempting to trap Jesus. Jesus wrote on the ground; they pressed Him for an answer; He stood up and presented them with a challenge that the first one without sin—sin in general or the same sin that she had committed—should cast a stone. (Incidentally, where was the man who had committed adultery with her? Where was he? Why hadn't they brought him?) Jesus stooped down again and wrote on the ground—whether something they could read or simply "doodled" we do not know.

They left. Then Jesus and the woman who had been caught in the act of adultery were left alone, facing one another. When He asked about her accusers, her word was that they had gone. Not one of them accused or condemned her. Then those wonderful, revealing words of Jesus, "Neither do I condemn you; go, and do not sin again" (John 8:3-11). In other words, Jesus did not whitewash sin. She had sinned. But this illustrates Jesus' attitude toward the sinner, whom He loved, and the sin, which He condemned.

Thief on the Cross

Another example of the fact that Jesus separated the sinner and the sin was what He said to one of the thieves who was crucified with Him. The thief said, "Jesus, remember me when you come in your kingly power" How did he know Jesus? And Jesus replied to him, "Truly, I say to you, today you will be with me in Paradise" (Luke 23:42-43). Where and what is Paradise may be debated; but the fact is that wherever Jesus was going to be after death that condemned and crucified criminal would be with Him. The thief on the cross may have been the last person to speak with the earthly Jesus and the first among millions to experience the saving power of the cross of Christ.

Mary Magdalene

There is another striking case of one who evidently had been a terrible sinner who was not only accepted by Jesus but mightily used by Him. The Gospel of Luke says that Mary Magdalene had had seven (the number of completeness) demons or devils cast out of her (8:2). Some have even suggested, which is doubtful, that she was the woman who anointed the feet of Jesus with her tears and the ointment she had brought into the house of Simon the Pharisee. One reason some conclude that Mary was the woman of the street who anointed the feet of Jesus in Simon's house is because she is spoken of immediately following the incident.

Whatever may have been the nature of Mary's sin, she evidently had had seven devils or evil spirits cast out of her by Jesus and in appreciation became one of Jesus' most devoted followers. She was one of a small group of women who, at least at times, traveled with Him and His disciples and helped to provide for their material needs. We can be sure that they were present at times when He spoke to His disciples as well as people in general and when He performed some of His marvelous miracles.

This Mary was one of the women who stood by when Jesus was crucified and when most of the disciples disappeared or followed at some distance. She, with some other women, watched where He was buried and came to anoint His body. Jesus first appeared to her after the resurrection. When Jesus, with a distinctive inflection in His voice, called her name, Mary recognized Him. To this one out of whom seven devils or demons had been cast, Jesus first spoke and through her sent a message to the twelve (John 20:11-18). In Mark's Gospel, there is an interesting addition. According to Mark, when Mary and the other women had come to the tomb to anoint the body of Jesus, they saw a young man dressed in a white robe. He assured them that Jesus had risen. His word was, "Go, tell his disciples and Peter that he is going before you to Galilee" (Mark 16:7). (It is generally supposed that Mark got much of the material for his Gospel from his close association with Peter. The two words "and Peter" must have been a source of great comfort and strength for Peter.) Jesus trusted Mary Magdalene, who evidently had been a very wicked woman, with His first message after His resurrection.

Saul of Tarsus

Space will not permit more than a brief reference to Saul of Tarsus, who became Paul, the major contributor to the formulation and early spread of the Christian movement. Who other than Jesus would meet on the way to Damascus a person who had persecuted Christians and was en route to Damascus for that purpose? But Saul, the persecutor, met the Master face-to-face. Saul did not know who or what had stricken him blind. His question was, "Who are you, Lord?" "Lord" frequently simply meant "Sir." The reply came clearly. "I am Jesus, whom you are persecuting" (Acts 9:5). Saul was blinded, but the inner eyes of his soul began to open.

When Ananias, following the instructions of the Lord, entered the house where Saul was staying, he laid his hands on Saul and said, "Brother Saul, the Lord Jesus who appeared to you on the road by which you came, has sent me that you may regain your sight and be filled with the Holy Spirit" (Acts 9:17). The one who had come to persecute became the persecuted. Can you imagine what might have happened to the Christian movement if Jesus, the Christ, had not separated the sin of Saul from Paul, the potentially outstanding formulator of the early Christian movement?

We should all cry in unison, "Thank you, Jesus, that you met Saul on the way to Damascus and began the process of making him into Paul, the dynamic preacher, teacher, and writer!"

The Twelve

In addition to these examples of the capacity and the fact that Jesus separated the sinner and the sin, brief attention must be given to the inner circle of Jesus' disciples— *twelve* whom He called in a special way to be with Him.

Relatively early in His public ministry, Jesus "went out into the hills to pray; and all night he continued in prayer to God. And when it was day, he called his disciples, and chose from them twelve, whom he named apostles" (Luke 6:12-19). The names are given. These were chosen to share with Him in a way and to a degree that was not true of Jesus' other followers. These apostles had the privilege of listening to Him as He taught the people but also in the more intimate conversation of close friends. Doubtlessly some of the most meaningful conversations occurred when they walked with Him over the dusty roads of Palestine. At times they may have slept out under the stars and listened as He spoke of the Father's world.

But who were those men who had that rare privilege of intimate conversation with Jesus? Other than the fishermen brothers—Peter, Andrew, James, and John—and Matthew, the tax collector, little is known about most of them.

We are aware that they were in many ways just ordinary men with weaknesses and plagued with the temptations of others around them. It does seem that, because of their close relation to Jesus, they became subject to a continuing and distinctive temptation. When Jesus referred to or talked about a Kingdom that was distinctly different from earthly kingdoms, the disciples seemingly could not or at least did not understand. Most of the time they evidently thought in terms of an earthly kingdom. This was the background for a debate they had from time to time about who was or would be the greatest in the Kingdom.

This debate may have centered around some of the more prominent of the apostles, such as Peter and John and their brothers, Andrew and James. It is very doubtful if some, such as James, the son of Alphaeus, Simon who was called the zealot, Bartholomew, and others would think of themselves as being the greatest in the Kingdom that they expected Jesus to set up.

On one occasion, the disciples had a dispute in the presence of Jesus about who would be greatest. They may have even asked Jesus' opinion. "He said to them, 'The kings of the Gentiles exercise lordship over them; . . . But not so with you; rather let the greatest among you become as the youngest, and the leader as one who serves. . . . I am among you as one who serves' " (Luke 22:24-27). This is an emphasis found over and over again in His teachings and demonstrated in His life. The great serve! On another occasion, He succinctly said, "He who is greatest among you shall be your servant" (Matt. 23:11; for similar emphases, see Matt. 18:1-4; Mark 9:33-35; Luke 9:46-48).

One of the twelve requires special attention in this chapter on the Jesus and the fact that He separated the sinner and the sin. When Jesus predicted that the disciples would be scattered or fall away, Peter had said, "Though they all fall away because of you, I will never fall away.

. . . Even if I must die with you, I will not deny you" (Matt. 26:33-35; see Mark 14:29-31; Luke 22;33; John 13:37). But Peter, as Jesus had predicted, denied Him three times before the cock crowed.

After the resurrection, Jesus had a meal with some of the disciples (John 21:1-23). Notice the question He asked Simon Peter after breakfast, "Simon, son of John, do you love me more than these?" A few days earlier, Peter had said, "Even though they all fall away, I will not. . . . If I must die with you, I will not deny you." Now, Simon, in the light of what happened at the time of my trial, do you still claim that you love me more than these others? Peter's answer was: "Yes, Lord, you know that I love you."

The second time Jesus asked Peter if he loved Him, Jesus left off "more than these." The third time Jesus used a different word for "love." The first two times he had used a form of *agapaō*. It describes a self-giving love that can be equated with God (1 John 4:8,16). The third time Jesus used the word that Peter had used—a from of *phileō*. It is descriptive of a love of friend for a friend. Jesus seemingly was saying, "Are you sure, Simon, that you love me even on that level?" It is possible that that was the reason, along with the repetition of the question three times, that "Peter was grieved because he said to him the third time, 'Do you love me?' "

Now impetuous Peter, who had boasted of his devotion to his Lord but who under pressure had denied Him three times, was ready to be used of the Lord. Peter, who had sinned terribly, was the one who preached that powerful sermon on the day of Pentecost and became the leader in spreading the good news among the Jews. The former sinner became a choice instrument of God. So the Christian movement has continued through the centuries. Great sinners, at least from time to time, turn out to be great saints. When this happens, it is the working of the grace of God, but a grace that can be operative only because our Lord separated the sinner and the sin, loving the sinner without condoning or ignoring the sin.

What about you, me, and other contemporary disciples of Jesus? Aren't we deeply thankful that Jesus continues to separate the sinner and the sin? It may be that we have not committed what is generally condemned as a terrible sin. But are we deeply conscious of sin in our lives? We should be grateful that our Heavenly Father forgives us and continues to use us in various ways in His work in the world. Thank you, Father.

Conclusion

In conclusion, let us meditate on a couple of quotations. These will be followed by two or three familiar hymns that have been quite meaningful to me and I trust to some of you.

David Moberg:

Moral condemnation of sin should not be confused with condemnation of the person who sins. He remains a person created in the image of God, one for whom Christ died. . . .

Some sins are more obvious than others, but this is not an acceptable basis for a legalistic self-righteousness that stands in the way of accepting the person who sinned. . . . God loves men as they are. Love imparts the hope of personal renewal to its recipients. Just as God became flesh and dwelt among men in order to communicate with man on his own level, Christians must go to people on their own level in order to reach them.[2]

Walter Russell Bowie:

Jesus, who knew what was in man, had a perception more

inclusive than that which contemporary Christians have. With his unclouded realism he knew the weaknesses and sins in human nature, but he did not stop with these. He saw, and brought into expression, the little glimmerings of goodness which may exist under the surface of a life that looks unpromising. His sympathy was like a divining rod which made him know where the answering waters were. In the world of today there may too often be cynical disparagement of human possibilities. What is needed instead is the power of the larger expectation that was always the mark of Christ.[3]

Favorite Hymns:

Do you have some favorite hymns or gospel songs? One of my favorites is the invitation hymn used on most occasions at the close of a Billy Graham sermon, "Just As I Am." It was also the song being sung when I gave my heart to the Lord as a sixteen-year-old and allowed Jesus to come into my life.

Many other hymns may come to your mind. Recently, in checking through an old church hymnal, the following favorites—more or less closely related to the emphasis we have been attempting to make—were noted: "Blessed Assurance, Jesus Is Mine"; "Christ Receiveth Sinful Men"; "Grace Greater than Our Sin"; "He Is So Precious to Me"; "My Jesus, I Love Thee"; "The Nail-Scarred Hand"; "O for a Thousand Tongues to Sing"; "What a Friend We Have in Jesus"; and "Whosoever Will."

Why not check through your hymnal and discover some of your favorites?

Let's return to the two Scripture quotations that are guiding our study:

By this we may be sure that we are in him: he who says he abides in him ought to walk in the same way in which he walked (1 John 2:5-6, author's italics).

It is only when we obey God's laws that we can be quite sure that we really know him. The man who claims to know God but does not obey his laws is not only a liar but lives in self-delusion(1 John 2:5-6, Phillips, author's italics)

How much of the spirit of Jesus is revealed in our attitude toward people who sin—Christians and non-Christians? How typical is our attitude to that of most of the members of our churches?

Notes

1. Walter Russell Bowie, *The Compassionate Christ* (New York: Abingdon Press, 1965), p. 202.

2. David Moberg, *Inasmuch* (Grand Rapids: Wm. B. Eerdmans Publishing Company., 1965), p. 117.

3. Bowie, pp. 300-301.

10
Who Is an Authentic Christian?

Why should the question, Who is an authentic Christian? be asked? Is it not sufficient to say that one is a Christian? Unfortunately, that is not enough. Some who claim to be Christians do not show much evidence in their lives that they have been made "new creations" in Christ Jesus. Really, you and I may have concluded from the study of our Bibles and meditation regarding the kind of life Jesus lived that few, if any of us, are authentic Christians. This conclusion may result to a certain degree from a clearer understanding of what it means to be an authentic Christian.

Another factor underscoring the need for a consideration of the question, Who is an authentic Christian? is the prevailing superficial manner members are voted into most churches. This is too frequently true, even of those who come by profession of faith. Entirely too many churches give little attention to the training and maturing of the ones who have professed their faith in Christ as Lord and Savior.

Even if we have had genuine experiences and are unquestionably Christians, there is still a very legitimate and necessary question that should be asked, Are we better or more authentic Christians this year than last year, this month than last month, today than yesterday? In other

words, in what direction are our Christian lives moving?
Or, are they moving at all? What is the direction of our
lives? Our Heavenly Father might judge us more by the
direction of our lives than by where we are. He might also
judge His children, at least to some extent, by the speed
with which they are moving toward increasing spiritual
maturity. Many may continue to be "babes in Christ"
when they should be fully grown men and women.

Inadequate Answers

Let us list and make a few brief statements regarding
several inadequate answers to the question of this chapter. We may correctly conclude that every one of these
should characterize a good or authentic Christian, but
that no one or even all of them provide a completely
satisfactory answer to the question, Who is an authentic
Christian?

Now, let us briefly suggest some of the inadequate answers:

1. Authentic Christians are ones who are *good moral
persons.* They pay their bills, maintain good credit ratings,
are honest in all of their business dealings, have reputa-
tions as good neighbors, do their best to live in accord
with the Ten Commandments and to follow the Golden
Rule.

2. Authentic Christians are *regular in church atten-
dance,* present every time the church doors are open
unless providentially hindered.

3. Authentic Christians are those who *support liberally
the work and program of the church, giving faithfully.* At
least, they tithe the family income and make from time to
time liberal special offerings.

4. Good or authentic Christians are *actively involved in
the work or program of the church,* teaching Sunday

School classes, serving as officers in some organization or group of the church, and supportive of the total program of the church and of the elected leaders of the church.

5. Authentic Christians are *witnessing Christians,* seeking to win the unsaved to faith in Christ, to enlist the unenlisted in the area served by the church.

6. Authentic Christians are *ones who are orthodox in their theology or beliefs,* sound in what they believe concerning God, Christ, the Holy Spirit, humanity, sin, salvation, the church, and so forth.

7. Authentic Christians are *ones who have dedicated their lives to some phase of vocational religious work:* pastor, missionary, and the like.

Most of the preceding inadequate answers are vital aspects of genuine Christian living. I say "most" because number seven should be restricted to those who have felt a special divine call. I regret to say it, but the fact that one has responded to a special call of God to enter some phase of vocational religious work does not necessarily assure that that person will live an authentic Christian life.

Although, as suggested above, the inadequate answers should and will characterize a good or authentic Christian yet not one, or even all, of them represent an adequate answer to our question.

Unfortunately, some Christians attempt to make one or several of these inadequate answers a complete or adequate answer. Too frequently, the answer to the question, Are you a good or an authentic Christian? will a be citation of one of the above: "I attend regularly," "I support my church," and so forth. In other words, often, verbally or otherwise, one or more of these inadequate answers is cited as a complete answer.

I could list many cases that would illustrate the last statement. A prominent member of a church did a great deal of personal witnessing to unsaved men and women and to those who were inactive Christians. He was a rather successful real estate dealer. Without being asked to do so, he started the practice of welcoming people at the front door of his church as they came to Sunday School and the worship services. Many of the people who had had business dealings with him went to the side doors to enter the church building, thus avoiding shaking hands with him. When the pastor discovered what was happening, he asked the man to stop welcoming people as they came in.

A Christian wife had finally gotten her non-Christian husband to attend the worship service of her church with her. On the way home after the service, he commented to his wife, "If the fellow who took up the offering in our aisle is representative of your church membership, I want no part of it."

Then, I share an experience that comes close to home for me. My older brother, Red, a successful businessman, did not become a Christian until after he retired. I remember a time when he was a young man that our grand old daddy and I were talking to him about becoming a Christian. I will never forget one statement he made to us referring to a deacon and the Sunday School superintendent of our church. He said, "Your 'Brother —' does some things in his business that I, a non-Christian, will not do." He spelled out specifically what he had in mind.

An Adequate Answer

I am not sure whether the statement should be singular, answer, or plural, answers. More than one adequate answer will be suggested. We may decide, however, that those answers in the main are different ways of saying the same thing. Possibly there is no more adequate answer than to say that real or good or authentic Christians are ones who let that which was a potentiality in their initial Christian experiences become a vital, dynamic reality in their lives. Can you remember your experience when you accepted Christ? Some great Christians cannot. They cannot go back to the time and place. I have been deeply grateful for an experience that has been a stabilizing factor in my life through the years. I am sure I did not understand then and still do not understand fully what happened that night in Smithwood Baptist Church, then a small country church but now a thriving suburban church of Knoxville, Tennessee.

I had been under rather deep conviction for several days. We had been on a football trip, and one of our players had been seriously injured. He had been left behind in the hospital at Asheville, North Carolina. We were uncertain whether he would recover. On the way back, the question plagued me: "What if that had been you? You are not ready to die." You may think that was somewhat morbid, but you do need to remember that this was the thinking of a sixteen-year-old. Also, it was many years ago when some of our reactions varied somewhat from those today.

The next week, as I walked to school and came back home after football practice, the struggle continued. As the Lord would have it, there was a revival meeting at our church. Each evening when my dad and sister would prepare to attend the revival, one or both of them would ask me about going with them. I would give them the excuse that I had to study. On Friday evening, they asked me the same question. I could not alibi that I had to study, and we did not have a football game the next day.

That night I went with them. My math teacher was the pastor of our little church and the preacher for the revival. I do not remember anything he said, but I can never forget the invitation hymn they sang: "Just as I am, without one plea,/But that thy blood was shed for me,/And that thou bidd'st me come to thee,/O Lamb of God, I come. I come." That hymn is to be used at my funeral. The one who presides is to explain why. My viewpoint for many years has been that it is just as appropriate at the end of the Christian life as it was at the beginning.

I did not understand then, and I am not sure that any of us can fully comprehend all it means to be a child of God. However, I can never forget the thought that came to me two days later as I was on my way to Sunday School and the worship service of our church. I can visualize exactly where I was when the thought came to me: *These two days with Jesus have been worth more than all the rest of my life.*

One way I have expressed what happened that night is to say that the resurrected Christ came on the inside of my life to live. Paul said something about Christ in you, the hope of glory (Col. 1:27). If that is correct, then for me to live a real or authentic Christian life means to let what was a potentiality when Jesus came in become a dynamic reality in my daily life. This is true for any child of God. Although our initial and subsequent Christian experiences may vary considerably, Christ in us is not only our hope of glory but is also the hope for a more fruitful and a more authentic Christian life.

Martin Luther said, "We are named after Christ, not because he is absent from us, but because he dwells in us, that is, because we believe in him and are Christs one to another and do to our neighbors as Christ does to us." This reminds us of the statement of Kagawa, quoted previously, that "Christians are little Christs." To the degree that we let Christ live in us and express Himself through us, to that degree we are real or authentic Christians.

The chapters we have studied together have sought to set forth, admittedly in an imperfect way, some of the qualities that characterized the life of Jesus as He lived in the flesh. Your review of at least the titles of the preceding chapters and the key Scriptures that have been used will help to answer the question, Who is an authentic Christian? An authentic Christian is one who permits the resurrected Christ to live in and through him or her.

This would mean, among other things, that an authentic Christian will go about doing good. To the degree that he does this, he will reveal Christ and hence reveal God. He will be concerned about people—all colors, cultures, and classes—but he will have a particular interest in and concern for the poor, the hungry, the handicapped, the underprivileged in general.

Think through the content of the other chapters and attempt to visualize what it would mean to your life and my life and to society if all of us who claim to be Christians honestly attempted to follow the teachings and example of Jesus. For example, who are the Samaritans for you and me—the individuals or groups of people whom we tend to avoid or ignore? How does our life-style compare to that of Jesus?

What place does ministry or service have in our daily lives? How broad and deep is our compassion for people, particularly people who hurt? Is our concern and compassion broad and deep enough to cause us to reach out and touch people, and particularly people who hurt? How effectively do we and our churches separate the sinner and the sin, being concerned for and loving the sinner without justifying or overlooking the sin?

How can we summarize what it means to be an authentic Christian? One way is to suggest that the outer expressions of his or her life will be a natural, almost inevitable result of what he or she is inwardly. In other words, the external and internal aspects of life will be compatible with each other. Another way of saying the same thing is that what he or she does accurately expresses what he or she really is.

Another characteristic of an authentic Christian is the fact that he or she will have a deep sense of having been sent. He or she will have a deepening consciousness of the challenging words of the resurrected Christ: "As my Father has sent me, even so I send you" (John 20:21). The fact that Jesus had a deep sense of having been sent by the Father gave Him a sense of "holy urgency." "I must" was rather frequently on Jesus' lips. "We must work the works of him who sent me, while it is day; night comes, when no man can work" (John 9:4). Why not take time to glance through the Gospel of John and notice how many times the words *send* and *sent* are found?

Jesus had a profound sense of having been sent to do the Father's will. He said to the disciples, "My food is to do the will of him who sent me, and to accomplish his work" (John 4:34). The deeper our consciousness of having been sent, the stronger will be our conviction that we, like Him, should do the will of the Father.

Jim Wallis said, "People should be able to look at the way we live and begin to understand what the gospel is all about. Our life must tell them who Jesus is and what he cares about."[1]

Martin Luther summarized the Christian life as follows:

> We conclude . . . that a Christian lives not in himself, but in Christ and in his neighbor. Otherwise he is not a Christian. He lives in Christ through faith, in his neighbor

through love. By faith he is caught up beyond himself into God. By love he descends beneath himself into his neighbor.[2]

The last portion of this statement, "descends beneath himself," is particularly relevant for our emphasis on a ministry that reaches down, or better, out to people who suffer and are underprivileged in general. Such a child of God seeks primarily a downward rather than an upward mobility.

Closing Confession and Commitment

Will you join me in confessing that you and I fall far short of being the kind of Christians we should be? The apostle Paul said:

> Not that I have already obtained this or am already perfect; but I press on to make it my own, because Christ Jesus has made me his own. Brethren, I do not consider that I have made it my own; but one thing I do, forgetting what lies behind and straining forward to what lies ahead, I press on toward the goal of the prize of the upward call of God in Christ Jesus (Phil. 3:12-14).

Can we and do we join with Paul in the last portion of that statement? These verses are full of athletic concepts: the effort of the runner, the goal of the race, and so forth.

How much progress have you made in the Christian life? I not only ask you that question, but I ask myself the same question. If we will seek as best we can to mature in Christ and no longer be babes, then we will increasingly be authentic Christians. Are you willing not only to confess that you fall short but also to join with me in a fresh commitment to a more accurate and fuller portrayal of the kind of life we are supposed to live as children of God? Will you join with me in a commitment that we will attempt as best we can to open our lives more fully to the indwelling Christ and give more of an expression of the kind of life He would have us live in every relation of our lives: in our churches, in our homes, as neighbors, where we work, and everywhere we touch people? Will we seek as best we can to be a good representative of the Christ who has saved us and seeks to live in and through us?

I know very little about music; I cannot carry a tune, but the good Lord has put some chords somewhere within me that enable me to be moved deeply by the playing or singing of a great, familiar hymn. There are times when I could weep, and occasionally do, when the choir or congregation of our church sings an old, familiar hymn. I may even be similarly affected when the organist or pianist plays the offeratory if it is something reasonably familiar and is not played too loudly.

Permit me to mention a few favorite hymns that are more or less closely related to the emphases of the preceding chapters. One of my favorites that is not closely related to the preceding chapters is "What a Friend We Have in Jesus."

One familiar hymn which is more directly related to the emphasis of the preceding chapters is "Make Me a Channel of Blessing," which is a request or prayer. Another, which is an admonition, is "Help Somebody Today." A stanza or two of it can and should be challenging to you and me:

> Look all around you,
>   find someone in need,
> Help somebody today!
> Though it be little—
>   a neighborly deed—
> Help somebody today!

> Many have burdens
>   too heavy to bear,
> Help somebody today!
> Grief is the portion
>   of some ev'rywhere,
> Help somebody today!

Still another favorite, which is a hope and a prayer, is "More Like the Master." The following is the third stanza:

> More like the Master I would live and grow;
> More of His love to others I would show;
> More self-denial, like His in Galilee,
> More like the Master I long to ever be.

The chorus of a song with a similar emphasis is as follows:

> Be like Jesus, this is my song,
>   In the home and in the throng;
> Be like Jesus, all day long,
>   I would be like Jesus.

Can and do you and I make the hope and prayer of the preceding hymns our sincere hope and prayer? Why not review some of your own favorite gospel songs or hymns?

Heavenly Father, we want to thank You again for the salvation we have through our union with the resurrected Christ. Help us grow in our understanding of what all it means to let Him live in and express Himself through us. Help us increasingly to go about doing good, walking as He walked or living as He lived. Forgive us for falling so far short of doing what we should do and being what we should be. This is our prayer in the name of Jesus, Your Son and our Lord and Savior. Amen.

By this we may be sure that we are in him: he who says

*he abides in him ought to walk in the same way in which
he walked* (1 John 2:5-6, author's italics).

Notes

1. Jim Wallis, *The Call to Conversion* (San Francisco: Harper and Row, Publishers, 1981), p. 108.
2. Martin Luther, *Selections from His Writings,* John D. Dillenberg, ed. (Garden City, N. Y.: Anchor Books, Doubleday and Co., Inc., 1961), p. 80.